LOOKING FOR *REAL* ANSWERS TO TEEN PROBLEMS?

Here's a book that will help.

Salt and Light: Talks and Writings on the Sermon on the Mount

Order Your Copy Now.

Yes. I would like to order **Salt and Light.**

☐ Please send me ___ copies at $6.00 each (add $1.00 for postage and handling).

☐ Check enclosed.

☐ Please bill me.

U.S. Senator Mark O. Hatfield: "The question of **Salt and Light** is whether we are loving God with our whole heart, mind, and soul, and loving our neighbor as ourself. Eberhard Arnold poses this question with inspiration and gentleness and creativeness."
—from the foreword

Thomas Merton: "Salt and Light has all the simple, luminous, direct vision into things that I have come to associate with Eberhard Arnold. It moves me deeply. It is the kind of book that stirs to repentance and to renewal. I am very grateful for it."
—Thomas Merton

Please make out all checks to the Plough Publishing House. Donations are tax-exempt. Canada and overseas, please pay in U.S. dollars.

Name ____________________

Address ____________________

City ____________ State ____ ZIP ________

PLACE
STAMP
HERE

Plough Publishing House
Hutterian Brethren
Ulster Park, New York 12487

PLACE
STAMP
HERE

Plough Publishing House
Hutterian Brethren
Ulster Park, New York 12487

PLACE
STAMP
HERE

Plough Publishing House
Hutterian Brethren
Ulster Park, New York 12487

For Additional Copies of A Straight Word...

Just fill out this card and drop it in the mail.

Yes. I would like to order additional copies of this teen help booklet.

☐ Please send me ____ copies of **A Straight Word...** at $3.50 each postpaid (or whatever you can afford).

☐ Check enclosed. ☐ Please bill me.

In addition, I would like to make a donation to the Plough Publishing House so that this booklet can get out to more people.

☐ Enclosed is a check for __________ .

Please make out all checks to the Plough Publishing House. Donations are tax-exempt. Canada and overseas, please pay in U.S. dollars.

Name ______________________

Address ______________________

City ____________ State ____ ZIP ________

THE PLOUGH magazine

Yes. I'm interested in hearing more from the people who published this booklet.

☐ Please send me a sample copy of your magazine, The Plough.

☐ Please sign me up for a free subscription to The Plough.

☐ I've enclosed a check as a donation to The Plough to help defray printing and mailing costs.

☐ Please send me ____ copies of **Freedom from Sinful Thoughts** at $3.50 each. (Add $1.00 for postage and handling.)

☐ Check enclosed. ☐ Please bill me.

The Plough magazine. talking about:

- peace and nonviolence • helping others • prison ministry • Christian community • education and family • tough issues facing the Church • more

Name ______________________

Address ______________________

City ____________ State ____ ZIP ________

Please make out all checks to the Plough Publishing House. Canada and overseas, please pay in U.S. dollars.

A Straight Word to Kids and Parents

Help for Teen Problems

Edited by the Hutterian Brethren
Artwork by Jdern Lybrand and Stevie Moore

PLOUGH PUBLISHING HOUSE
Hutterian Brethren
Ulster Park, New York, USA
Robertsbridge, England

A Straight Word to Kids and Parents
Help for Teen Problems

First printing: 10M June 1987
Second printing: 10M July 1987
Third printing: 10M December 1987

Library of Congress Cataloging-in-Publication Data

A Straight word to kids and parents.

Summary: A collection of Christian readings which offer advice on such topics as drugs, dating, television watching, suicide, and crime.
1. Youth—Conduct of life. 2. Youth—Religious life. [1. Conduct of life. 2. Christian life]
I. Hutterian Brethren (Rifton, N.Y.)
BJ1661.S87 1987 241'.04973 86-30360

ISBN 0-87486-186-1 c10 1287

Contents

Introduction

DEAR FRIENDS,

Don't try to read this book from cover to cover as a novel—it isn't. Don't look for total answers to the problems addressed in this handbook—you won't find them. This book is only a beginning. And after all, the real answers can only be found in the depths of your own heart.

IF YOU'RE IN HIGH SCHOOL, chances are that in the past week your parents spent 14 minutes communicating with you. Dad and Mom have been replaced by an electronic teacher and guardian—the flickering tube.

PARENTS. TEACHERS. COUNSELORS. MINISTERS. The moral fiber of our society is dangerously frayed. Our kids are hurting. One-third of them between the ages of 18 and 25 use drugs like cocaine, heroin, and PCP, and two-thirds have tried marijuana. Around 3.3 million kids between 14 and 17 are considered acute problem drinkers, and 20 to 25 people will die today in alcohol-related crashes. And if you read in the paper that Dick Jones down the street has been arrested for murder, rape, child abuse, armed robbery, or dope peddling, you can be sure he will be sitting in jail watching the same crimes on TV.

We may think our high hopes for Johnny are part of our love for him, but that is not how he sees it. To him it's pressure for good grades and a spot on the varsity squad. He needs to know we love him regardless of his "achievements." Does the stereo or new car we give our kid show our love, or does it say, "stay out of my hair"? Where does our time go—to a career that only brings in money for more steroes and cars? Is Johnny getting a message that says, "You live your life, I'll live mine," leaving him to cross the street and join the gang? And then we're outraged when he calls from the city jail—"Yeah, I'm charged with D.W.I. Can you drop by the hospital and see how my girlfriend's doing?"

The burden is on us. Kids need to find the joy and self-respect that come from doing something for somebody else, of helping someone worse off than themselves. They need a purpose for living. And they need our love, not gimmicky substitutes.

TEENS. You have a responsibility to the next generation. You have to get your life established before you enter a serious relationship. And you can't call it marriage if it's not serious. Fifty percent of American homes are being destroyed by split-ups. Are you going to add to that? Don't hand your kid hell to grow up in. A child needs a two-parent home, a mother's steady faithful tenderness. A child needs to be able to come and say, "Dad, I got a problem," and know he'll get a listening ear. A child needs to feel wanted, to have a place in life, to feel roots that give him security.

MAYBE YOU'LL ONLY READ one of these chapters. Maybe you'll only flip through and look at the pictures. But I hope that if you get only one thing out of this book, you'll learn that for any problem you may face, others have been there and found a way out. *There is a way out.*

—Daniel Moody

Daniel Moody is a member of the Hutterian Brethren and lives at the Woodcrest Bruderhof in Rifton, New York, where he is a minister and director of the Brothers' Prison Ministry.

JESUS CAME TO BRING HEALING to man's innermost life through His blood. Every heart, however tormented, can find comfort in the thought of the Cross and the healing that issues from it.

—Heini Arnold

This and later excerpts by Heini Arnold are taken from the book Freedom from Sinful Thoughts, *available from Plough. Heini Arnold was an elder of the Hutterian Brethren for 20 years until his death in 1982.*

TELEVISION

TV Robotics
Are You in Control of Your Life?

by Sibyl Sender

A MAN WHO WORKED FOR 15 YEARS as an advertising executive said of TV, "I learned that it is possible to speak through [TV, radio, magazines] directly into people's heads and then, like some otherworldly magician, leave images inside that can cause people to do what they might otherwise never have thought to do."

The man's name is Jerry Mander. He knows there are thousands of men and women whose job is making people crave specific material things. Once they can get you to watch TV rather than, say, jog, they've won half the battle. Once you're glued to the tube, they make you think you *must* have a deodorant, or a beer. From there, the scramble is to make you buy *their* brand of the thing you think you can't live without. It's a fearful thought to them that one or two people might slip through the net knowing perfectly well that life is rich and wonderful without these things.

But let's go back to that first step—making you want to watch TV. How do they do it? A little box with flickering images. How can it be that we look at it for hours on end—while real life passes us by? Well, we've been studied, and every person in the TV business knows exactly how to cement our attention to the set. With *action.* And what's

more active than violence?

That is why there is so much violence on TV. The advertisers buy time on the violent programs because it's so hard for people to stop watching it. Not many advertising people stop to think that the show can sell your soul on violence as effectively as the commercial can sell your flesh on beer. Many people think every minute of TV watching is a kind of hypnosis—you and the rest of us are being programmed to buy, buy, buy . . . and to be violent, sexy, domineering, powerful, and lots of other things we might not want to be, deep down in our hearts.

Shaping peoples' characters through national drama began back in the 1930s. Today there are many middle-aged adults who say they were brainwashed by movies long before TV was invented. These older people are still doing things they'd rather not do because of the remote control effect of movies on their lives as children. Take cigarette smoking. Millions of Americans wish they'd never begun it. But for years every movie they saw pictured people smoking. Now, several generations are hooked into a habit they'd like to kick but "can't."

Perhaps each person says to himself, "But I am different. I have my own values, and nothing I watch or read about can affect them. Just because I see a story about killing your grandmother doesn't mean I'm going to rush right out and do it too."

True enough. But each person *has* done things he wishes he hadn't. And the influence of television on your values is very subtle. You don't even know your attitudes are slowly changing.

Let's say you intend to be a good, decent person, trustworthy and friendly and wholesome. If you were offered an all-expenses-paid scholarship to the University of Murder, Arson, and Rape, would you accept? If someone invited you to the worship services of a heathen idol would you attend?

Of course not.

But the truth is that if you are an average American you have already graduated from the Preschool of Pornography, the Elementary School of Ultimate Horrors, the Junior High of Junk, and you're working on a Ph.D. in Violence Unlimited. You have spent more time learning how to live like a criminal than you have in learning anything else your school teaches. That's because during your school years you have spent an average of three hours at the set for every two in the classroom.

Your home has become a temple, your family the congregation, and the TV set the chanting priest of a religion of vileness. You have attended more worship services than a Trappist monk. You thought you were being entertained, but actually you were being preached to.

The tube has been your school and your religion; it may even have been your mother, your father, your sister, and your brother—because you listened to it far more than to any of them. So the tube is your family too.

I don't need to tell you what comes out of the tube. You

> Not many advertising people stop to think that the show can sell your soul on violence as effectively as the commercial can sell your flesh on beer.

know. You know that its values are not your values in most cases. But you can't stop watching. You feel you should not spend all your time watching the wretched stuff, but *you can't stop.* Can this be true—that thing is stronger than you? This is the case with many adult, educated, respectable people—they are confessed TV addicts.

A heavy viewer (a college English instructor) observes:

"I find television almost irresistible. When the set is on, I cannot ignore it. I can't turn it off. I feel sapped, will-less, enervated. As I reach out to turn off the set, the strength goes out of my arms. So I sit there for hours and hours."

If you are an average American you have already graduated from the Preschool of Pornography, the Elementary School of Ultimate Horrors, the Junior High of Junk, and you're working on a Ph.D. in Violence Unlimited.

Marie Winn, who wrote a book on TV addiction in kids, says:

"The self-confessed television addict often feels he 'ought' to do other things—but the fact that he doesn't read and doesn't plant his garden or sew or crochet or play games or have conversations means that those activities are no longer as desirable as television viewing. This is one reason people talk about their television viewing so ruefully, so apologetically. They are aware that it is an unproductive experience."

I wish I could believe it was merely "unproductive." I suspect, and many others suspect, that it is very productive. It produces things that no one really wants: homework that is left undone, relationships that die of neglect, lives empty and wasted. In extreme cases TV produces or stimulates criminal behavior. Certainly if I were the warden of a jail or prison, I would not sit my wards before that teacher of violence and mayhem for months on end.

What if you are tired of being a TV robot, tired of being told what you need to buy, how you should pull out a gun to solve problems, rape or mug the people who get in your way?

There are people who have, one way or another, broken their enslavement to the tube. Several of their stories are detailed in Marie Winn's book, *The Plug-In Drug*. In every case TV freedom is simultaneous with a life of discovery.

In one example, a storm blew down and broke the TV aerial. Later, inside the house, four children sat in a row on the long sofa in the living room, staring at the empty place where a television set had stood. They sat there for quite a while. "It was pathetic," their mother reported. "For a few weeks they wandered around like lost souls." These children lived in a large farmhouse surrounded by woods and fields in northern New York State, a paradise of fishing streams, wildlife, recreation.

Their parents never fixed the aerial. Today those children are different kids. They even notice it themselves. They talk about their friends as "indoor kids who don't do many interesting things." Now the kids spend all their time outside. "But it took time," says their mother, who was herself addicted. "You can't just turn off your set for a few days and expect anything to change much. It takes time to get television out of your system."

People have discovered that getting a normal amount of sleep at night enriches the whole person, as does eating leisurely meals laced with good conversation. Families have had time to get to know each other's problems and talk about them. For the first time they begin to feel they and not the "stranger in the home" are in control.

So take another look at your life. Are you becoming a TV robot who eats and sleeps and views as the master commands?

Let's say you decide to cut the umbilical cord between you

and the set. How are you going to do it? Remember, it is not enough to say "I won't watch it." You've got to avoid the presence of any operating TV set because once it is operating, its effect is as good as hypnotic.

Jerry Mander, in his excellent book, *Four Arguments for the Elimination of Television*, asked three prominent psychologists, famous partly for their work with hypnotism, if they could define the TV experience as hypnotic. Mander described a typical viewing as a "dark room, eyes still, body quiet, looking at light that is flickering in various ways."

Dr. Freda Morris said, "It sounds like you're giving a course outline in hypnotic trance induction."

Dr. Ernest Hilgard said the above conditions would be "the prime component in the induction [of hypnosis]."

Dr. Charles Tart was not sure if hypnosis was the exact word for it but the conditions would induce an "altered state of consciousness" since they disrupted the pattern of ordinary awareness and then offered a new patterning system to put back together the broken pattern. In other words, the TV image is injecting a powerful drug into your brain that messes up the way you think.

It's scary to think what might happen if TV fell into the hands of people with evil intentions. Or maybe it already has. Here's what a Russian visitor to the United States said of the television he had seen while here:

"Frankly, I could hardly believe my eyes when I was in the United States—the kind of things you showed on television. If the things you show are representative of the kind of life you have in America, God help you! All the killing and beatings and cheating and swearing and wife-stealing and immorality! A nation can't help being judged by the things it's interested in.

"But what is most surprising to me is that you apparently have no idea of the kind of harm this is doing to your children. They sit in front of the TV sets for hours at a time and take it all in. What kind of food is this for tender young minds? And you wonder why you have a juvenile delinquency problem."

Maybe it hurts to hear such strong language from an "outsider." But I think he's on to something.

So, you have to get away from your set or get your set away from you. Refusing to fix the broken set is one of the most successful escape routes. But if it's not broken, there are many ways to get rid of a television set. Just don't give it to someone else.

A few like-minded people could start on this adventure together. In Denver, 15 families volunteered to go without television for at least a month and keep diaries on the difference in family life during that time. According to them,

There are many ways to get rid of a TV set.

you'll feel weird the first few days. Call it withdrawal symptoms. But then the advantages start to pour in.

Now, what to do with that ocean of time that spreads before you? Country dwellers can go after nature as a whole, or concentrate on one aspect of it. City dwellers might try a museum or a zoo. Take up photography, learn a musical instrument. Remember, since your hours before the tube were utterly profitless, you don't have to worry about "wasting time" with what you do with your "new" time. Since you were not being paid to watch TV, you don't have to be paid for what you do with the time now. This brings up an interesting possibility. Say you're interested in cars—you might find a mechanic who would listen to your tale and let you get the feel of his shop through volunteer work. Of course, any nonprofit group like a hospital or day care center will gobble you up.

You could show people this article so they know what's bitten you. Start a diary and you'll surprise yourself. Document your "withdrawal symptoms," discoveries, adventures. Write to us and tell us your story, now that you're liberated. We'd like to hear about it . . . and print it.

Sibyl Sender came to the Hutterian Brethren from Madison Avenue, New York City's publishing and advertising center. She spent a weekend at the Bruderhof community to prove that her atheism could not be shaken—and lost the bet. Or won, depending on how you look at it. Her brothers and sisters can testify that 30 TV-less years have not marred her character in any way.

IT'S 1983. The world is preparing for Christmas. Hollywood is also prepared. The nation has been blitzed by a new film, *Silent Night, Deadly Night.* "Silent Night" is no longer the calm, bright night surrounding a virgin mother and child. In a short moment one sick mind has turned Christmas from a warm family experience to a crazed Santa Claus descending a chimney, ax in hand, to butcher the occupants.

IT'S 9:00, SATURDAY NIGHT. The newly painted corridor stretches down the tier past 16 cells. Midway down the cellblock, a television is bolted to the ceiling. With arms draped over the bars that separate them from the set, 20 inmates are staring, mesmerized.

I can feel it in the air. Tense. Electrified.

As I approach the crowd, I can see the screen. The shadow of a man crosses the screen. The camera switches. A woman in a laundromat. A switch back to the man, now flattened against the wall, treading cautiously, muttering under his breath. The camera plays on his face, distraught, wild eyes. He is going to murder. Back to the woman, at work in the laundromat. She is about to be murdered.

One of the inmates starts chanting under his breath, "Kill her! Kill her!" It's picked up by the others. "Kill her! Kill her! Kill her!" Louder and louder.

WHAT ARE WE DOING TO OUR YOUNG PEOPLE? What are we feeding these young men? I had come to hold a meeting next door in the jail library to try to help these men understand that there is a better life for them. That there is hope for them and for their loved ones at home. But how can I compete with the lies they're getting for hours on end every day on TV? Isn't it time for a radical new look at today's TV programming?

—Daniel Moody

NATURAL EMOTIONS OR IMAGES in the fantasy can frequently be traced back to earlier impressions on our feelings. This fact is an alarming warning about the evil effects that movies, newspapers, television, and so on can have. Why is this state of affairs allowed to exist with no warning of the awful consequences? It brings ruin to the souls of little children, a ruin often caused by the indolence of parents or teachers.

—Heini Arnold

DRUGS

The Innocent Drug

by David Toma

THIS COUNTRY IS IN TROUBLE. There's an epidemic raging, and we can't pretend it isn't happening. There is hardly a family that will escape its poison if we don't wake up to the danger and begin to fight it.

While the adults in this country have been obsessed with improving their lot in life, *the kids have been sucked into the most insidious drug culture that has ever existed.* Drugs are warping their values, crippling their bodies, killing their minds.

Plenty of adults are going to say that I'm exaggerating, crying wolf, all black and white. Well, here's an invitation to everyone who reads this. Spend one day with me in any school where I'm speaking—elementary, junior, or high; city or suburban; public or private. Listen to what the kids tell me about drugs and alcohol. The critics become believers fast. They may not accept what I say, but they'll believe the children.

And the kids will know what I'm talking about; that's what matters most to me. They are the ones I love and want to help.

> This country is in trouble. There's an epidemic raging, and we can't pretend it isn't happening.

MARIJUANA IS THE MOST POPULAR DRUG in America today, and kids are the biggest users. It's cheaper. It's easy to use. Lighting up isn't as scary and ugly as putting a needle into your arm. Pot parties are friendly, social, ritualistic. So what's the big deal?

Marijuana contains one of the most destructive chemicals found in any drug . . . and it doesn't leave your body when you blow the smoke out of your lungs. The technical term is delta-9-tetrahydrocannabinol. You may know it as THC.

When people say that pot is less dangerous than alcohol it's because they don't know about THC. Alcohol is water soluble. THC is fat soluble. As soon as it gets into the body it heads for the fatty tissue—and enters the fat cells. THC gets locked into the cells of your brain, your liver, your kidneys, your glands, and in your reproductive system. This drug is so potent that if you use it just once a month you have an active, poisonous chemical operating in your body 24 hours a day. And, my friends, if you're smoking one joint a week you are a heavy drug user.

What will the THC do to you? Your memory will be one of the first things to go. Kids tell me that it gets so bad that they don't remember their phone number and address.

And thousands of kids have told me that from marijuana alone they experience numbness in various parts of their bodies. Sometimes it lasts for a few days, sometimes for months, and some say it never leaves them.

And when the pot-sickness gets so bad that you can't get through the day without being high, then the idea of suicide begins creeping into your mind. Kids tell me every day that suicide becomes an obsession with them.

Marijuana is unpredictable. One plant can contain up to 60 times as much THC as the plant growing next to it. And you don't know which one of the joints in your pocket has the power to blow you away.

Everywhere I go kids come up to me and want reassurance. "Mr. Toma," they say, "I been smoking pot for three or four years and so far nothing's happened to me." Don't kid yourself. You're playing with a killer, and there's no telling when it will hit.

There has never been a scientific study that concludes that marijuana is safe. But there have been hundreds of studies that show that marijuana is harmful. Dr. Robert DuPont is one of the experts who used to think that marijuana is "less of a hazard to health than tobacco or alcohol." Dr. DuPont was the director of the National Institute on Drug Abuse when he made such statements.

Well, Dr. DuPont was wrong about marijuana, and he has had the courage and honesty to admit it. In 1978 he was quoted in the *Washington Post:*

"I get a very sick feeling in the pit of my stomach when I hear talk about marijuana being safe. Marijuana is a very powerful agent which is affecting the body in many ways."

Dr. DuPont caught up with the research in 1979, and I'm sure that he's been staying on top of it ever since. But too many experts avoid the research as though it didn't exist.

There's a myth about marijuana that has to be shot down—that marijuana doesn't lead to other drugs. I've rarely met a kid who uses speed, LSD, heroin, dust, cocaine, mushrooms, who didn't start off with marijuana. The more pot they smoke, the more they need to get a good high. So when they are offered some other drug that promises a good high they don't care what they have to put into their bodies to get it.

And don't get the idea that I take any other drug lightly. The others are killers too. Especially alcohol. It's just that marijuana is the most misunderstood street drug.

The pressure on kids to use dope is tremendous. Drug users love to turn other kids on. It makes them feel safer.

"I get a very sick feeling in the pit of my stomach when I hear talk about marijuana being safe. Marijuana is a very powerful agent which is affecting the body in many ways."

The kids who aren't doing drugs are considered freaks. And the teachers are rarely any help to the kids who try to resist. Too many of the media idols use dope and don't keep it a secret.

I know what the pressure's like. I've gone through this a million times. I'm having dinner with someone who doesn't know me very well, and the waiter wants to take an order for cocktail or wine. I ask for soda or juice, and my dinner partner tries to coax me into having a highball. He doesn't want to drink alone, he says. What does he think I'm planning to do with my tomato juice? Eat it with a fork? It's weird. He doesn't insist that I put pepper on my salad or gravy on my mashed potatoes, but he sure is uncomfortable if I don't put scotch in my soda.

Millions of adults are alcoholics and plenty of them have children. And plenty of kids tell me that their parents do drugs. What chance do they have? Most parents who read this will say, "Hold it, Toma. I'm not an alcoholic. I don't get high on drugs. I don't beat my kids. I love my children. I'd give them the shirt off my back. If my kids get into drugs, it's because of outside influences. The world has changed since I was a kid. It's tough to raise a child in a world that seems to have gone crazy."

Friends, it has never been easy. It wasn't easy for my parents or millions of other immigrants who came to this country penniless, uneducated, and unable to speak the language. They managed though, and they didn't lose a generation of children to drugs or alcohol. And it wasn't easy during World War II, when our country was turned upside down and families torn apart. We survived somehow, and the children didn't turn to drugs and alcohol. So what's happening now? Why do kids from decent homes prefer the dangerous drug culture to the straight world?

If you are going to raise an emotionally healthy family, you have to get your values in order. You have to know where you and your wife and your kids fit into your life—and where your career and the things that you are struggling to acquire fit in. It's more difficult to be a successful mother and homemaker than it is to become a successful business person.

If you are part of a two-parent family, the greatest gift you could ever give to your children is to make sure their mother is home when they come home from school. In my family, dinnertime is when we're all together. That meal is an event, even if we're having leftovers.

The caring parent makes it a point to know what's happening to his child. The child needs his parents for support and guidance and love. If he doesn't get this from his parents he'll get them from someone else, and the price he may have to pay can be incredibly high.

My kids know that if I see them getting out of line, I'm going to intervene. I have to—I'm their father. I love them. But my kids know what it is to be spanked. I've restricted their activities—and I've cut off their allowance. But I never ignored them or gave them the silent treatment. And I never laughed at them when they were serious, or belittled their feelings when they were angry or jealous or frustrated.

A friend of mine told me about a conversation he heard between a 16-year-old girl and her parents when he was visiting their home.

The girl raced through the living room and headed for the door.

Father: Where are you going?

Daughter: Not sure.

Father: Who are you going with?

Daughter: You don't know them.

Mother: What are you going to do?

Daughter: Hang out.

Father: When are you coming home?

Daughter: I have a key.

Mother: Do you have enough money with you?

Terrific! I guarantee you that if that was one of my daughters, she would never have made it through the door. I'd never put up with that kind of nonsense, and my kids know it.

From what I see, we have slopped together a lazy, self-centered society. We can blame a lot on government, big business, labor, inflation, and the energy shortage, but the problems begin in the home. With the family. And the family starts with a marriage. Almost every marriage is a trial marriage, and about half of them fail.

It's pretty tough to keep a family whole when the parents operate as two free independent individuals, each one seeking "personal fulfillment." Kids feel like their situation is temporary. I've listened to enough kids to know that more youngsters get into drugs—and can't get out—when their family life is shaky and there are serious problems with their parents' marriage.

There is one alternative to the way too many people are living today. It's a family headed by a husband and wife who are committed to make their marriage work—who can express their love and give their children a sense of worth. Kids need to grow up in a lifestyle that includes the teaching and demonstration of morals, values, and responsible behavior. And I'm not embarrassed to tell you that God and the sharing of a religious experience is part of the Toma family lifestyle.

Kids who are given "things" in place of loving attention feel unloved. Do you believe that? Kids need to be hugged and kissed and told that they are loved. Kids need to know what behavior is acceptable and what behavior is unacceptable by their parents. What is unacceptable? Tantrums, lying, cheating, disrespect, meanness, smoking pot, popping pills, having premarital sex. And they need to know that rules must be obeyed, are sensible and predictable, not arbitrary and changing. Why is the number one complaint that I hear from kids always the same? They feel unloved, unwanted, unnecessary.

How to know if your kids are doing drugs and how to help them stop

A few of the kids I talk to say their parents know about it but don't care. But most honestly believe that their parents have no idea that they are doing drugs. Believe me, *your child has been exposed.* There's no such thing as too young.

Look for changes in your child's behavior. They begin to worry. They're afraid of saying the wrong things that might tip them off. They avoid conversations. They spend time in their room or visiting friends. They turn down family activities. Some parents misread the signs. "Hey, the kid's growing up! Gotta give him some space." They may mean well. But they're just stepping back when the child needs his family the most.

Once a kid becomes a regular pot smoker he usually splits

from his non-pot-smoking friends. The new friends may talk more hip jargon, appear unkempt, meet behind closed doors, record player blasting. He's less likely to bring any of his friends around. Phone calls become more mysterious, callers are less likely to leave their number. Pot smoking is almost the only thing on his mind. It's tough for him to hold down a part-time job. His grades suffer. Their short-term memory seems to be short-circuited. Pot smokers become accident prone, and turn into terrible (and dangerous) drivers.

They may complain of numbness in the limbs and torso and the side of the face. Pink eyes and sensitivity to light are common symptoms. The smoker often coughs, wheezes, and complains of chest pains. Marijuana can throw off a girl's regular menstrual cycle. You'll see big mood swings in a heavy pot smoker. I've known kids who smashed furniture, broke windows, and busted holes in the walls with their fists. He may become suspicious and fearful to the point of paranoia. And, of course, there's the physical evidence: pipes, cigarette papers, incense, eye drops, roach clips, locked boxes and drawers, drug-culture magazines; pills, seeds, and stems found in pockets and purses. When a kid always needs money you can worry. And when he seems to have too much money you can worry, too.

No one wants to spy on his children, but every parent needs to know. Your child needs you to know. If your kid is on drugs he or she needs you desperately.

The number of elementary school kids who smoke marijuana and drink liquor is growing at a frightening rate. Teachers can help if they know that the parents really care. Don't allow a teacher to diffuse your concern by minimizing the dangers of pot. Find out how the school handles its drug problem. If you're told there is no problem, somebody's sleeping. You want drugs out of the school, and you want to be sure that there is never a whitewash of it.

If you are not certain about your children, then you have to do everything possible to find out. You probably won't get the truth out of a regular user. But if your child denies using drugs and you have no reason to suspect he's lying, accept his answer. Your kid is going to be pressured to use drugs throughout his school years and needs you to help keep him on the right track. You know enough now to stop it in the early stages.

Many of you know right now that your child is into drugs. More than ever he needs you now. First of all, don't panic. If you punish yourself with a heavy guilt-trip, you'll be useless to your children when they need you the most. You may feel hurt and betrayed. You may suffer, but you'll survive. You may feel uncontrollable anger. But when you deal with your children it must be with strength, compassion, and love.

Confront your kid as soon as possible, when you don't have one eye on the clock. Keep him out of school and take off work. Both parents should be present even if you are divorced, if that's possible, and both in complete agreement on your approach. He must know that if he doesn't turn off drugs the consequences will be enormous, not only in terms of his health, but what you, as the parents, will and will not do for him from this point on. Your approach has to be straightforward. Quitting drugs—that's all you will talk about. So let your kid know what you know—lay it all out in front of him. Then brace yourself.

> Why do kids from decent homes prefer the dangerous drug culture to the straight world?

Your child's first reaction will probably be one of indignation, even outrage. Don't let him throw you. You did what you had to do. The odds are that he will deny using drugs. Don't believe it. No matter what evidence you have he will probably swear that they don't belong to him. Do you know how many parents buy that story? Plenty. At this moment, your kid will say anything, promise anything, to get you off his case. What you must do will turn your son's or daughter's world upside down. He will be separated from his

If you are part of a two-parent family, the greatest gift you could ever give to your children is to make sure their mother is home when they come home from school.

pot-smoking, pill-popping friends. He will give up the feeling of being high.

Your child must know that you are prepared to contact the parents of his friends, to speak to his teachers and the school principal, to be notified any time he misses a class and is absent from school. He must know that you will find out who the pushers are and that you are prepared to notify the police and the school administrator.

Until you are convinced that he is free of drugs you won't permit him to drive a car. Take his driver's license away from him, now. Until he is clean of drugs, you won't give him any money or credit cards. If he has a bank account, take the pass book. If he needs school supplies, you buy them.

You must know where he is day and night. You'll give him a curfew and you want to see him when he comes home. You will periodically inspect his room. The kid must be given responsibilities and chores in the household. His room should be clean and so should he. The point is, you have to break the pattern in his life that has been so damaging.

A kid who is exhibiting the symptoms of a heavy pot user should be kept under close observation for about 60 days—to get the THC out of his system. One of the parents should be with him continually during this period. It's an agonizing and expensive option, but if the child blows his mind the cost will be astronomical. He'll feel trapped. He may be explosive, vile. Never stop loving him and never stop hating the drugs.

If you can keep your child away from pot for two months, you'll see a dramatic change in his behavior, and he'll understand and appreciate what you have done for him.

Too many parents are willing to make compromises along the way. If their relationship with the child improves within a couple of weeks, they let their guard down. Don't do it, no matter how tempting. I can't tell you how important it is to stick to your program until the kid is absolutely free of the drug poison.

What can you do if the child is in his late teens, full grown, and completely out of control? You must take steps that may shatter that kid's world. You may have to call the police. You may have to commit him to a mental health facility. And you may have to put him out of your house. All of these options are traumatic ones and must be considered only as a last resort. If your kid is a heavy pot smoker, you don't want him in a facility where they will give him tranquilizers or any psychotropic drugs. You must find a place that understands the damage that marijuana does to the user.

You can't allow an 18-year-old boy or girl to destroy the rest of the family. Try not to order your kid out when you are furious with him, and don't close a door on him that may be impossible to open. But he must know that unless he's able to live in your house under strict rules set down by you, he must leave. It's a risk, but if you let such a kid stay home, on his terms, there is no risk—you are sure to lose him.

The four basics are:

One—You've got to be straight yourself—you can't be playing the game that you're telling other people to quit.

Two—You've got to know what you're talking about. They'll

never respect you if you talk about drugs without real understanding.

Three—You have to care and show them that you love them and are genuinely concerned for their welfare.

Four—You must have the patience of a saint. Never, never give up.

Kids—I'm counting on you to quit drugs NOW!

I'm writing this because I love you. What I see happening to you terrifies me. Organized crime has zeroed in on you. They don't care if they kill you. They'll replace you with your little brother and sister.

If you're playing around with drugs and alcohol, you are a danger not only to yourself but to everyone you come in contact with. I want your parents to intervene in your life. I want them to do everything in their power to stop you before you destroy yourself or someone else.

All users think they are in control. The mental hospitals are full of these people. And the prisons. Almost every violent crime committed by a teenager is drug- or alcohol-induced. And the graveyards are filled with the bodies of young kids who thought they were in control.

A while back I visited a jail in New York. I walked through the cell block with a cop I've known for years. A kid in one of the cells called to me.

"Mister, I gotta talk to you. I need help, please talk to me."

"What's the problem, son?" I asked. "What can I do for you?"

He lowered his voice so my friend couldn't hear.

"I've been here seven days already, and they won't let me call my father. Please, I'll give you the number. Call my father. Tell him I'm in trouble. I need him."

He was in trouble all right, but his father would never be

able to help him.

The cop told me the story. This boy was a nice kid, never been in trouble before. College student, upper middle class. He smoked marijuana but wasn't considered a heavy smoker. A couple of months ago he was hit with angel dust. Someone had stuffed a joint that he smoked with it.

After the party, he walked into the house where he lived with his family, took a gun out of his father's desk drawer, went into his parents' bedroom, and killed them both. Then he killed his little sister.

He doesn't know they're dead. He doesn't remember killing them. He had been in jail two months and every day he cries for his father to come and help him.

Marijuana. The innocent drug. The fun drug.

EVERY KID WHO LIGHTS UP A JOINT TODAY is a potential pusher. It doesn't matter how nice you are or how gentle you are. You can't predict how the poison's going to affect your behavior. And when you become a pusher, my friends, you are one of the most dangerous animals on earth. You are directly responsible for damaging the minds and bodies of kids who probably consider you a friend. Pushers should be avoided as though they were lepers. I have talked to thousands of pushers in my life. I haven't met one yet that I didn't end up caring for. But that doesn't change the fact that I don't want them around my loved ones.

Most pushers didn't intend to go into the business. It just happened. Like the last one I talked to. Only once did she hint to her dealer that she wanted out, and his reaction terrified her.

"I want to quit now," she told me. "I never thought about the kids I was selling to. I didn't know anything about drugs except they get you high. But how can I quit? He'll kill me. I know he will."

Drugs can kill you in a hundred ways. Your parents have

to know that. Make up your mind, today, that regardless of what anyone else does, you are going to save yourself. No one can do the job for you.

I wouldn't sit on a panel with a sex offender and argue the pros and cons of rape. So don't argue with anyone who uses drugs. If they are willing to listen to you—fine. But don't listen to them.

I don't want this country to be handed over to a generation of potheads and alcoholics. So don't get angry at me for trying to get your parents involved in your life. If you're lucky, I'll reach them and someday you'll thank me.

There is only one way to quit and that's cold turkey. There is no such thing as tapering off. You can't have one last hit "for the road." You just quit. Quitting requires action. Get rid of all the junk that you have stashed away. Now start calling your closest friends. Tell them that you'll never get high again and that you have to break away from those who do.

If your parents know you were doing drugs, or suspect it, call a family conference. Tell them that you quit. Talk to your teachers and principal. If there isn't any anti-drug program in your school, urge them to start one. More than anything else, stay away from the drug users and pushers. Walk, run, exercise. Get into music, sports; drink a lot of fluids—water, fruit juices—no alcohol. Much of the garbage and poisons will be removed from your body by the exercise and fluids.

Be patient with yourself, especially if you have been heavy into pot. It will take time for all the THC to work its way out of your body. In time your ability to concentrate, read, and comprehend will improve. And so will your schoolwork. Your relationship with your parents will certainly improve. Try to be a positive force in your family.

I don't know what you kids are going to do when you finish reading this. Plenty of you will quit drugs, but some of you won't. I can't force you to quit. I'll pray for you though. I'll pray that if I failed to reach you, someone else will get to you before you blow your mind forever. It doesn't matter, at this point, why you started using drugs. You didn't know what

There is only one way to quit and that's cold turkey.

you were doing to yourself, but now you know. You can never again be innocent of the facts. If you continue now, you have no respect for life.

Let me know how you're making out. I promise that I'll read your letter. Write to: David Toma, P.O. Box 854, Clark, NJ 07066.

I love you. I'm not ashamed to tell you. I love you all! And God bless you.

David Toma began his study of the drug problem as a detective in Newark, New Jersey's, vice, narcotics, and gambling division. His ruse of self-disguise enabled him to penetrate every level of the drug culture. David talks with thousands of teenagers all across the country each year, and he's had a brush with addiction himself; he knows what he's talking about.

Where to Go for Help

- Toll-free Numbers:
  Cocaine Helpline 1-800-COCAINE
  Action/Pride National Drug Information Hotline
  1-800-241-9746
  Substance Abuse Center 1-800-443-5744
  National Federation of Parents for Drug-free Youth
  1-800-554-KIDS

- Every state has a central agency for all the drug abuse, prevention, treatment, and rehab programs within that state. To contact the agency in your state, call your state capitol and ask for the Department of Alcohol and Drug Abuse.

- Also, every state has a central ACTION agency for all the volunteer programs in that state. To get the phone number of your state ACTION office, phone your state capitol or contact: ACTION, 806 Connecticut Ave., N.W., Washington, DC 20525, (202) 634-9135.

- The National Clearinghouse for Drug Abuse Information, which is operated by the National Institute on Drug Abuse, will provide the latest information on drugs, prevention, and treatment free of charge. Write: National Clearinghouse for Drug Abuse Information, 5600 Fishers Lane, P.O. Box 1706, Rockville, MD 20857.

- Your community pharmacist knows about drugs and their effects on you. He is concerned that drugs are not misused. Contact him for information or advice.

***IN THE STRUGGLE OF THE HEART** that does not want to have anything more to do with evil, the "will" can do very little, and often, very often, produces the opposite result. If we hate evil in the depths of our hearts, then we must seek to build upon something deeper in our hearts than our own "willpower."*

When in spite of evil thoughts, ideas, and images we really want God and Christ in the deepest core of our hearts, it means that Christ** is **deep within our hearts.

—Heini Arnold

ALCOHOL

A Spreading Epidemic

WE FIND THEM at cocktail parties or at church, in an executive office suite or behind the door of our own homes. In increasing numbers, they attend our local high school. They are middle-class, rich, and poor; white, black, Spanish, and Indian. Some are melancholy, some euphoric; some are angry, others docile. They worship in synagogues, cathedrals, large evangelical churches, and small charismatic prayer meetings.

These men, women, and children—up to ten million Americans—have one thing in common. *They are alcoholics.* The intoxicating liquid which over a hundred million Americans drink for pleasure, they drink from necessity. Slowly but certainly, if left unchecked, they drink themselves to death, insanity, or institutionalization.

Only 5% of addicted drinkers live on skid row; the rest are our neighbors. Some are infants born with the smell of alcohol on their breath: alcoholic mothers are the number three cause of birth defects associated with mental retardation. Some are grammar school children: in Nebraska, boys and girls as young as eight years old are suffering from cirrhosis, delirium tremens (DTs), and other alcohol-related problems. Others are among the 3.3 million teenagers all over the United States who bounce back and forth between alcohol and illegal drugs. And a growing number are housewives, "hidden alcoholics" who secretly sip their lives away and baffle unsuspecting husbands with erratic, unpredictable behavior.

Sadly, neither doctors, mental health professionals, nor church members are equipped to handle this growing epidemic of addiction. The pronounced sense of helplessness with which our society approaches addiction is completely misleading. This pessimism in part accounts for why 90% of all alcoholics never enter treatment programs, but it overlooks the remarkable percentage of addicted drinkers who, *having received appropriate help*, are living sober, productive lives.

—Dr. Anderson Spickard
and Barbara Thompson

The Toll

ALCOHOLISM CAN AFFLICT ANYONE who drinks—but certain population groups show a greater incidence of the disease. The largest rate of alcohol abuse is found in urban areas, particularly in the northeast and on the Pacific Coast. Among ethnic groups, American Indians have the highest proportions of alcohol-related problems. Youthful problem drinking appears greater among upper-income groups than lower, and the majority of teenage abusers are either the children of alcoholics, come from a broken home, or have suffered physical or sexual abuse during childhood.

Statistics on alcohol abuse:

- Last year, the average American drank 22.4 gallons of beer, 1.85 gallons of wine, and two gallons of hard liquor. Eighty percent of the country's nearly 100 million drinkers have less than two drinks a day. The other 20% drink nearly three-quarters of all alcoholic beverages sold.
- The manufacturing of beverage alcohol is a $36 billion-a-year industry. Excise taxes on retail sales constitute the third largest source of federal revenue.
- One out of every five dollars spent in hospitals goes toward alcohol-related problems.
- Liver cirrhosis ranks as the sixth most common cause of death in the United States, with up to 95% of the cases estimated to be alcohol-related.
- Alcohol is implicated in a third of all suicides, half of all homicides, half of all rapes, three-quarters of all robberies, and half of all fatal car crashes.

—Michael Segell

"THE SOUL MUST LONG FOR GOD in order to be set aflame by God's love; but if the soul cannot yet feel this longing, then it must long for the longing." To long for the longing is also from God.

—Meister Eckhart
quoted in *Freedom from Sinful Thoughts*

Life With an Alcoholic

by Joanne Ross Feldmeth

"YOU WANT TO KNOW WHY I drink so much?" Tim had asked her the night before. "Just go look in a mirror, honey." And with a dry laugh, he had walked out of the house. In response, she stood motionless, fighting tears and hoping the children hadn't heard him.

This morning, however, Carol is determined to win Tim's approval—and stop his drinking—with an ambitious self-improvement campaign of her own. He apparently "needs" to drink, she reasons, in order to cope with the growing pressure over finances and the children's problems in school. Still, Carol is certain that if she can improve her looks and lessen the tensions around the house, Tim would drink less.

Will her plan work? "No; absolutely not," states Dr. Anderson Spickard with firm conviction. Spickard is medical director of the Vanderbilt Institute for Treatment of Alcoholism in Nashville, Tennessee. In his opinion, Tim's drinking pattern and his need for chemical help to face everyday problems tell Carol something she doesn't want to hear: her husband is probably an alcoholic.

Spickard warns that alcoholics drink not because their wives are frumpy or their children are slow in algebra or their checkbook balance is too low; they drink because they are in the grips of a compulsive disease. Many alcoholics are quick to blame their families for the problem—and they can be very convincing: sons, daughters, and spouses often accept the accusation that it is their fault. They think wistfully, *If only I could get better grades (or make more money or lose more weight), Dad (or Mom or my spouse) wouldn't drink so much.*

Guilt over "causing" the alcoholism can tear a family apart. As everyone alters their normal life to accommodate the drinker's habit, their own needs get pushed aside. They learn quickly that the alcoholism is not something they should talk about; it is a private shame. Soon thereafter, they do almost no honest sharing at all.

This drama is enacted in countless North American homes. More than 10 million Americans and 600,000 Canadians suffer from alcoholism or alcohol-related problems. The disease is the direct or indirect cause of 95,000 deaths annually in the United States alone. And for every person who suffers from alcoholism, another four people are directly affected.

"People need to be told that it is *not* their responsibility if someone else decides to drink," says marriage and family counselor Steve Powell of South Bay Hospital in Redondo Beach, California. Powell works with patients and their families in an in-hospital treatment program for alcoholism.

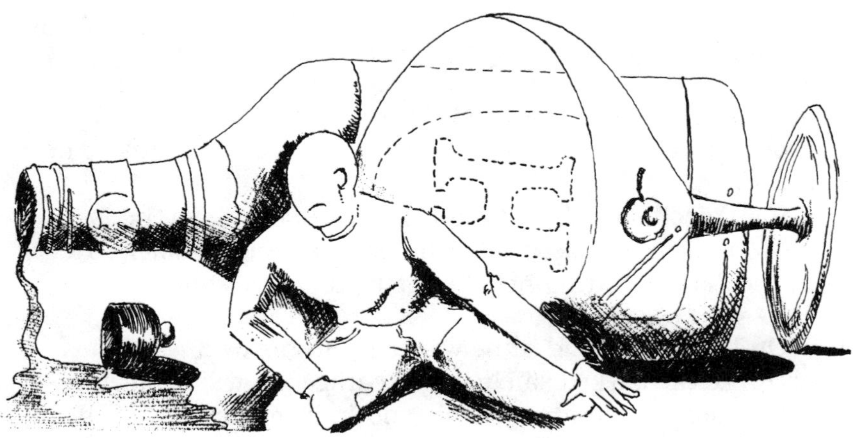

He says that a lingering sense of guilt and embarrassment traps families into assuming more and more responsibility for *all* of their loved one's actions.

For example, if an alcoholic drives home drunk and parks the car on the neighbors' front lawn, members of his family typically spring into action:

The wife helps him out of the car and into the house where he vomits on the rug. The daughter cleans up the mess while the son parks the car. By this time, the wife has managed to put her husband to bed. Then she apologizes to the neighbors ("John has been under a lot of stress at work lately . . .").

The family members are compassionate, loving, and Christian—and they are doing everything wrong.

Alcoholism treatment experts advise families in this situation to do nothing to help the alcoholic unless his personal safety is threatened. Powell says that once it is clear that no harm has come to the alcoholic, nothing should be done: "Don't clean him up. Don't put him to bed. Don't move the car. Don't apologize for him."

What's wrong with helping? Basically, says Spickard, that kind of "help" dulls the natural consequences of a person's alcoholism. "What is needed is tough love," he advises, "the kind of love that will keep someone from throwing his or her life away."

If an alcoholic sobers up on the neighbors' lawn, he is surrounded by evidence that he has a serious problem. He may consider getting help before he dies—or kills someone else—in a car accident.

On the other hand, if he wakes up in his own warm bed with the car parked safely in the garage, he will be far less interested in changing. He may not remember the episode at all, and will find it easy to deny its seriousness.

Of course, the alcoholic whose family decides to let him take responsibility for his actions may become enraged. "You have betrayed me!" sputtered one man tearfully to his family. "I needed you, and you let me down!"

Such a hard message is difficult for loved ones to hear. Compounding the problem, Spickard notes, are well-meaning clergymen who don't fully understand alcoholism and often counsel family members to keep meeting the alcoholic's expectations.

What is needed is loving, but tough, confrontation. It is very important to call someone who is experienced in counseling families of alcoholics; many physicians and family counselors have little background in handling such volatile situations. "This is critical," says Spickard. "Misdiagnosing can be tragic."

Alcoholics Anonymous is one of several organizations that can provide a support group needed while the patient is undergoing professional care. Even though a family may be convinced that their loved one should have treatment, he probably will not agree initially. In any case, family members need help and support in learning how to stop "enabling" the disease.

If the alcoholic balks, an "intervention" may be necessary—a carefully planned confrontation between the alcoholic and his family and friends. During a four- to six-week period, a counselor meets with the family members to help them recognize how the alcoholism has affected them and continues to damage their loved one, physically and emotionally. During these sessions, each family member prepares a list of specific instances during which he was hurt, embarrassed, or upset by the alcoholic's behavior. Angry, hurtful words must be replaced by bare, factual statements. Finally, the time for the actual confrontation is set.

Several guidelines are commonly recommended for staging such a confrontation:

—The intervention must be scheduled at a time when the alcoholic is sober.

—It is best held in a doctor's or counselor's office. The encounter should not be attempted without professional help.

—Incidents should be read aloud calmly from an approved script, with factual details and dates included. Joan reminded her husband: "The doctors thought I had cancer. The symptoms looked bad, and I was afraid. On June 12, however, you were not sober enough to drive to the doctor's office with me. I had no one to share my fear as I drove there. And when I got the results, I had no one to share my relief."

Joan's daughter read: "Dad, you were drunk on April 3d. It was my wedding day. It should have been a perfect memory, but you weren't sober enough to stand in the reception line."

—The alcoholic is then asked to take action, often by entering a hospital treatment program or by participating in daily Alcoholics Anonymous (or a similar group's) meetings.

By the end of the intervention, the subject is miserable. Scene after scene of his decimated-yet-destructive life has been flashed before him by those who care about him: his family, his minister, perhaps, or his best friend or employer.

Suddenly, the people who have been spending years keeping the problem quiet are *causing* a crisis.

"It's true that most alcoholics have to 'hit bottom' before they agree to enter treatment," explains Dr. George Patterson of Glendale (CA) Memorial Hospital. "But an intervention raises the bottom they have to hit. It feels just as hard, just as intense, but this way they hit bottom *before* they lose their job and their family. And they have an alternative of hope: treatment."

Accepting that option, however, is difficult. For years, the alcoholic has believed he could stop drinking by mustering up enough "willpower." But that alone cannot free someone who is locked into a physiological addiction. Determined, strong-willed personalities with this compulsive disease have no more control over their drinking than weaker-willed alcoholics.

Even if an alcoholic refuses treatment, his intervening family has taken an important step toward restoration: The truth has been told. The family has stopped shouldering the blame for their loved one's condition, and has stopped participating in his or her sickness.

Kate recalls that her father resisted every suggestion to seek treatment. But as his family continued to press him, he began to bargain: he would go—next month, maybe; well, OK, next week; finally, he agreed to enter the program that day. The family members burst into tears and shouts of congratulations.

Kate stood among her family that day, dry-eyed and strangely numb. "I knew that this was just the beginning of a long process," she said. "But after all those years, it was so important just to *begin.*"

Joanne Ross Feldmeth is a freelance writer living in Los Angeles.

Alcohol the Drug

IN SMALL AMOUNTS, alcohol acts on that part of the brain which controls inhibitions. It relaxes the restraints which govern behavior, giving the drinker a sense of well-being, or euphoria. This release of the emotions from their normal controls frequently causes alcohol to be mislabeled a stimulant. In fact, it is a depressant that slows down the intellect and other bodily functions.

In larger quantities, alcohol depresses the cerebellum and interferes with the body's balance mechanism. The drinker begins to stagger, and his speech becomes slurred. Because his judgment is seriously impaired, the drinker is usually unaware that he can no longer properly walk—or drive. For most people, two and a half drinks (approximately three to four ounces of alcohol) in one hour is more than enough to make driving a risky business.

In very large quantities, alcohol anesthetizes the brain stem, the body's control center for respiration and heartbeat. A fifth of whiskey in an hour is normally enough to paralyze completely the brain stem and send the drinker into an alcoholic coma. This lethal effect of alcohol is generally unknown. Every year a number of high school and college students are admitted dead-on-arrival to hospital emergency rooms because they accepted the challenge to chug-a-lug six-packs of beer or a fifth of vodka.

—Dr. Anderson Spickard
and Barbara Thompson

Paths to Sobriety

CURRENTLY there are three well-trodden and successful paths of treatment which help alcoholics find the holistic healing they need: 1) Inpatient treatment at an alcohol rehabilitation center, 2) Outpatient treatment, and

3) Alcoholics Anonymous (AA).

At the heart of AA's effectiveness is a 12-step program that gives a systematic account of how the founding members of AA gained their sobriety. While they are simple enough for the foggiest drunk to understand, they are also profound enough that any of us could spend a lifetime trying to practice them without exhausting their spiritual potential.

—Dr. Anderson Spickard and Barbara Thompson

The 12 Steps of AA

1 We admitted we were powerless over alcohol—that our lives had become unmanageable.
2 Came to believe that a Power greater than ourselves could restore us to sanity.
3 Made a decision to turn our will and our lives over to the care of God *as we understood Him.*
4 Made a searching and fearless moral inventory of ourselves.
5 Admitted to God, to ourselves, and to another human being the exact nature of our wrongs.
6 Were entirely ready to have God remove all these defects of character.
7 Humbly asked Him to remove our shortcomings.
8 Made a list of all persons we had harmed, and became willing to make amends to them all.
9 Made direct amends to such people wherever possible, except when to do so would injure them or others.
10 Continued to take personal inventory, and when we were wrong promptly admitted it.
11 Sought through prayer and meditation to improve our conscious contact with God *as we understood Him,* praying only for knowledge of His will for us and the power to carry that out.
12 Having had a spiritual awakening as the result of these steps, we tried to carry this message to alcoholics, and to practice these principles in all our affairs.

Drugs and the Alcoholic

THE MAJORITY OF ALCOHOLICS today are cross-addicted to one or more drugs—cocaine, marijuana, tranquilizers, hallucinogens, amphetamines—and it is important that all recovering alcoholics understand that they cannot stay sober and continue to use other addictive substances.

Teenagers in particular need to be warned that drugs and alcohol, when taken together, have a *synergistic* effect—the total impact of their mix is greater than the sum of their parts. Quantities of pills or alcohol which might be safe when taken by themselves can cause permanent brain damage or death when ingested together.

—Dr. Anderson Spickard and Barbara Thompson

The Honorable Alcoholic

by Harold E. Hughes
Former United States Senator from Iowa

WHENEVER A BOTTLE WAS PASSED AROUND, whether it was outside a country dance hall or in the rest room at a high school social, it stayed the longest with me. I drank because it lifted my inhibitions and made me relaxed and easygoing at dances and social affairs. When I took a drink I never wanted to stop.

I dropped out of college in my first year and returned to Ida Grove, Iowa, to marry Eva. She tried to keep me sober, but couldn't. After going off to war in 1942 and serving as a foot soldier through battles in Italy, I returned home with a thirst stronger than ever.

Was I alarmed about my craving? Definitely not—after all I worked full time as a truck driver who was never drunk on the job (see? I *can* control this thing!), and I brought home a paycheck every week. Who's being hurt by my drinking? "I can stop drinking whenever I want to."

After one particularly rough day I had a few shots and walked to my parents' home, where Eva and I were living. Mother was rolling out noodles. As I passed her, she evidently caught the odor of whiskey, set the roller down, and turned to me, pain in her eyes. "Harold, please," she choked, "Please don't come home like that . . ."

Rage filled me. I rushed into our bedroom, pulled out a fifth of whisky, stamped back into the kitchen and slammed the bottle down on the table so hard it foamed. "By God," I yelled, "I'll drink wherever I want to: I'm a man now, fought through a war for my country, and am sick of being treated like a kid!"

Turning, I rushed out of the house and roamed through the darkening streets, cursing myself for hurting Mother.

Incidents like this made me decide to stay sober from sheer strength of will. Once I managed to stay dry for over a year. And then a friend tried, tactfully, to steer me to Alcoholics Anonymous. Why not come to a meeting with him that night?

"Friend," I said smiling, "Thanks, but no thanks. I know you had a big problem, but mine isn't that bad. I'm able to handle it, and I don't need any club to help me do it."

But after falling "off the wagon" again, and then again and again, I decided that drinking was an inevitable part of my life and I no longer made claims about trying to stop. Instead, I shifted the emphasis to "control." But deep down I wasn't at all sure I could control my drinking.

A drum beat of doom seemed to fill my days and nights. I cringed at people's comments and knowing winks; at seeing the flush in my face in the mirror; at the deepening fatigue which racked my body. Yet I was powerless to stop doing the one thing that caused it all.

FOR SOME TIME I SAT IN THE CAR in our driveway not wanting to get out. A cold January wind moaned through the bare trees. The house looming before me was dark. And I sensed it was as empty as my soul.

I felt sure my wife and little daughters were gone. Eva had often left when she thought I'd be coming home drunk. Besides, we had a dinner invitation for tonight, one she especially hoped I would not miss. Now the dinner hour was long past and Eva had had to suffer the embarrassment of showing up without me.

Finally, I climbed out of the car and carefully made my way to the house. A tricycle clattered along the sidewalk when I banged into it, but I didn't sense any pain. Reaching the steps, I stood there for a moment, holding on to a rounded porch column.

Again, I had hurt the ones I loved so much. My head pounded in guilt and nausea. Slowly the alcoholic fog seemed to lift. As it did the sense of shame sank deeper into me. What was the point in going on any longer? I couldn't face Eva, the girls, our parents. I couldn't even walk downtown any more and meet the many good friends whom I had insulted during drinking bouts.

I found myself wandering about the house, a sense of blackness closing in on me. In the bedroom, I slumped onto our bed. I sat there, realizing the awful hopelessness of my condition. I couldn't control my drinking; for ten years alcohol had controlled me.

What was the point of living? I'd failed everyone who had meant anything to me; I was a disgrace to my town. I didn't go to church—that would be phony. I was a hypocrite in everything I did; I couldn't even tell the truth anymore.

I couldn't do anything right. Why not just end it?

The thought hung there, like the echo of a tolling bell.

I remembered enough Scripture to know that suicide was not God's way. But as I weighed the balance, I felt it better to be eternally lost than to bring eternal hell to those I loved.

No, my mind was clear now. I hated what I did, but I still did it. When I promised loved ones I wouldn't drink and even prayed to God that I wouldn't drink, and did it again and again, I realized in my heart that there was no way on earth I could ever control it.

I got up from the bed and went to the closet. I reached for the shotgun. It was a single barrel Remington pump gun, 12-gauge.

I considered what I was going to do to Mother, Dad, Eva, the children. Eva was still young. She could easily find someone else to marry and have a decent life. The thought

I hated what I did, but I still did it.

hurt me. The girls would eventually forget me. As I was then, they would never forget, suffering only disgrace and sorrow.

I slid three shells in the magazine and pumped one into the chamber. Tears streaming down my face, I walked into the hall and into the bathroom. It could be cleaned easier. Carefully holding the Remington, I climbed into the tub.

It was an old-fashioned claw-footed tub. The porcelain was cold to my hand as I stepped into it, my shoe soles squeaking on the tub bottom. I lay down. With the shot gun resting on my stomach, I positioned it with the muzzle in my mouth toward my brain. Reaching down, my thumb found the trigger.

A terrible sadness filled me. I knew what I was doing was wrong in God's eyes. Yet, my whole life had been wrong. And God had always been very remote. In a few years my family would get over it, I reasoned. They would have an opportunity to rebuild their lives. But if I remained here, I would never change and only hurt them more.

The thought came that I should explain all this to God before pushing the trigger. Then if He could not forgive this sin, at least He would know exactly why I was committing it.

Climbing out of the tub, I knelt on the tile floor and laid my head on my arms, resting on the cool tub rim.

"O God," I groaned, "I'm a failure, a drunk, a liar, and a cheat. I'm lost and hopeless and want to die. Forgive me for doing this . . ." I broke into sobs, "O Father, please take care of Eva and the girls. Please help them forget me . . ." I slid to the floor, convulsing in heavy sobbing. As I lay face down on the tiles, crying and trying to talk to God, my throat swelled until I couldn't utter a sound. Totally exhausted, I lay silent, drained, and still.

I do not know how long I lay there. But in that quiet bathroom, a strange peace gently settled over me. Something that I had never experienced before was happening, something far beyond my senseless struggles.

God was reaching down and touching me. A God Who cared, a God Who loved me, Who was concerned for me despite my sins. Like a stricken child lost in a storm, I had suddenly stumbled into the warm arms of my Father. Joy filled me, so intense it seemed to burst my breast. Slowly I rose to my knees and looked up to Him in the awe of gratitude.

For a long time I knelt there. Then I stood up, breathing heavily as if I had just climbed a long hill. Reaching into the tub, I picked up the shotgun. I unloaded the shells and placed the gun back in the closet.

I knelt at the bed: "Father," I prayed, "I don't understand this or know why I deserve it. For You know how weak I am. But I put myself in Your hands. Please give my family back to me . . . and give me the strength never to run again.

For a long while I knelt there. Then I climbed into bed, rested my head on the pillow and for the first time in months slipped into a deep, peaceful sleep.

Bright sunshine streaming through the window awakened me. An exuberance filled me, and then I remembered the night before. I got up and made coffee, thinking how close I had come to killing myself. I knew that if I drank again I would put myself under the control of dark forces that would lead me to the same horrible pit.

IT TOOK ONE MORE TERRIBLE COLLAPSE back into drunkenness to break down my stubborn resistance to the group that could have helped me from the beginning—Alcoholics Anonymous. Hesitantly I attended a few meetings. Finally, filled with respect for this little band of men who put their trust in a higher Power, I joined up. And with this step the specter of alcohol left our home. Permanently, I prayed. For I was really learning to live one day at a time.

In 1962, only ten years after his near suicide, Harold Hughes was elected governor of Iowa. At the end of his third term, Senator Robert Kennedy persuaded him to run for senator and swell the ranks of doves on the Vietnam issue. Throughout his term as senator from Iowa, Hughes felt increasingly called to surrender his life to the will of God, though it would mean "throwing away every material success I had struggled for." Though he was regarded as a possible presidential candidate, Hughes stepped out of politics at the end of his senate term to follow his inner calling. Since then he has dedicated his life to helping alcoholics through the Hughes Foundation.

A Sin—Or a Disease?

FROM THE CHRISTIAN PERSPECTIVE, alcohol abuse, or drunkenness, is clearly immoral. Alcohol abuse is involved in most murders, most assaults, most child abuse cases, most traffic fatalities, and most fire and drowning accidents. It is also a primary factor in the development of alcohol *addiction.*

But while the alcohol abuser chooses to get drunk, the alcoholic drinks involuntarily. Telling an alcohol addict to shape up and stop drinking is like telling a man who jumps out of a nine-story building to fall only three floors.

Because of the alcoholic's helplessness, and because addiction follows a predictable pattern and has a pronounced inheritance factor, it is not inappropriate to call alcoholism a disease. However, it is never simply a *physical* disease; rather, alcoholism is a disease of the *whole* person. The alcoholic is sick in his body, mind, emotions, spirit, and relationships. Unless he gets help in all areas, his chances for recovery are poor indeed.

After a profound conversion experience, I was eager to help my alcoholic patients by leading them into a personal relationship with God. I knew that if the Lord could rescue me from the bondage of pride and arrogance, he could rescue alcoholics from the bondage of alcohol. With a diagnosis in one hand and a Bible in the other, I could only stand and watch while my patients exhausted the last energies of their talented lives in pursuit of "just one more drink."

Only after 20 years of medical practice did I begin to learn that alcoholism responded to a specific program of treatment, and that over a million men, women, and teenagers all over the world were recovering from addiction. I felt stunned, as if I had spent years unsuccessfully treating diabetic patients with prayer and psychotherapy only to discover that thousands of diabetics were doing quite well by controlling their sugar intake and using insulin. It was a rude awakening.

Today, hundreds of alcoholic patients later, I am more convinced than ever that alcoholism is a treatable disorder.

Alcoholism, like diabetes, is a progressive chronic disorder which can be controlled or arrested, but is seldom cured. This is a stumbling block for some Christians. "I move in full Gospel circles, and I believe in healing because I've seen God heal," says an alcoholic friend. "But whenever I tell my friends I'm a recovering alcoholic, they say that's a 'bad confession.' They try to convince me that I'm not *recovering*, I'm *healed*. These friends mean well, but without knowing it, they pose one of the biggest threats to my sobriety. God has healed me from my burning compulsion for alcohol, but all my life I'm going to be just one drink away from a drunk."

—Dr. Anderson Spickard
and Barbara Thompson

The Unborn Child

NO ONE KNOWS how much alcohol a pregnant woman must drink to harm her unborn child. Even small amounts of alcohol (one-half ounce) can affect the breathing movements of a child *in utero.* Moderate daily amounts of alcohol (one ounce) have been shown to reduce a child's birth weight dramatically.

When a childbearing woman drinks alcoholically or heavily, there is substantial risk that her baby will be born with *fetal alcohol syndrome.* This disturbing cluster of serious and irreversible birth defects includes mental retardation, stunted growth, and odd facial deformities. It is the number three cause of birth defects associated with brain damage, and its occurrence increases every year.

The surgeon general of the United States has determined that there is *no* safe amount of alcohol a pregnant woman can drink. Unfortunately, a great deal of damage can be done to an unborn child in the first seven weeks of pregnancy, the time period when women normally are unaware that they are carrying a child.

The effects of alcohol on unborn children remain a strangely well-kept secret, and the price we pay as a society for this ignorance increases every year.

—Dr. Anderson Spickard and Barbara Thompson

Where to Go for Help

- Many people who treat addictive diseases find that the best road to recovery is through self-help groups modeled on the program developed by Alcoholics Anonymous. If you have an alcohol problem, contact them now. Their central office is at Box 459 Grand Central Station, New York, NY 10163, (212) 473-6200. To find the AA group nearest you, just look in your phone book under Alcoholics Anonymous.

- Another group offering help is the National Council on Alcoholism at 12 West 21st Street, 7th floor, New York, NY 10010, (212) 206-6770.

- For information and reading materials, contact the National Clearinghouse on Alcohol Information, PO Box 2345, Rockville, MD 20852, (301) 468-2600.

- Does the excessive drinking of a friend or relative affect you? Call Al-Anon Family Group at (212) 683-1771 or write Al-Anon Family Group Headquarters, P.O. Box 182, Madison Square Station, New York, NY 10159-0182.

- If you're a teenager and affected by the drinking of a family member or a friend, contact one of the 3,000 groups called Alateen, a division of Al-Anon, for help. Look up Al-Anon or Alateen in your phone book or write to Al-Anon's address.

DEEP IN OUR HEARTS IS JESUS. ***We must think about experiencing Him. This thought will then become reality when our hearts find the right detachment, that is, the right peace and quiet. If our hearts are not quiet, we will not experience Jesus. Even if He were to stand beside us, we would not notice Him.***

—Heini Arnold

DATING

Breaking Out of the Dating Game

by Tony Campolo

ASK YOURSELF THIS SIMPLE QUESTION: How many high school kids do I know who are hurting because nobody ever asks them out on a date? You can find kids in any American school every day who are hurting.

Whenever you create a system for teenagers that requires them to have partners of the opposite sex in order to participate, then you've created a social system or activity that automatically excludes a lot of kids. Furthermore, you end up excluding those who most need to be included. You close out those who are hurting the most. As Christians, we should be reaching out to the persons whom society rejects. Instead, we sometimes unconsciously support a system which fosters their sense of rejection.

If you go to a school with a thousand kids, the system

usually works for only about two hundred of them. Only two hundred out of a thousand get the praise, the strokes, and the recognition needed for a positive self-image. What about the other eight hundred who live their lives in "quiet desperation"? Shouldn't Christians be heartbroken over them?

A few years ago Janice Ian sold a million copies of a song. It was popular because it communicated the feelings of so many kids in America. Hurting teenagers listened intently whenever the song was played and thought to themselves, "That's me. That song is about me." The song goes like this:

> I learned the truth at 17,
> That love was meant for beauty queens
> And high school girls with clear-skin smiles,
> While those of us with ravaged faces,
> Lacking in the social graces,
> Desperately remained at home
> Inventing lovers on the phone
> Who called to say "Come dance with me,"
> And murmured vague obscenities.
> It isn't all it seems, at 17,
> For those of us who knew the pain
> Of Valentines that never came
> And those whose names were never called
> When choosing sides for basketball.
> It was long ago and far away,
> The world was younger than today,
> And chains were all they gave for free
> To ugly duckling girls like me, at 17.

The song tells it like it is, and we Christians should be aware of that. The American dating system is making kids hurt.

Jesus was committed to affirming those who were rejected by society. He didn't exactly choose the most popular and attractive people to initiate His involvement. He said, "From the stones the builder rejects will come the stones out of which I will build my new world."

The system tends to get young people to put a premium on personal traits and characteristics which, in the long range of life, prove to be superficial. On the contrary, a number of things that really count are ignored. The kids who make it in the dating system are usually good-looking, but may be shallow, while many quality people who aren't so good-looking don't stand a chance.

I know attractive, personable girls who graduate from high school never having had a date, and those dateless years so devastate their sense of self-worth that they find themselves saying things like: "I'm nothing. Nobody could love me." The consequences of such self-contempt can destroy a girl's moral standards. Show me a girl with a lousy self-image and I'll show you a female who is very easy to seduce sexually. A girl's self-concept has a powerful effect on her actions. If she thinks she's trash, she'll act like trash. But if she thinks she's a precious child of God, she will act like one.

We are supposed to be trying to tell people about the love of Jesus, and there is no better way of doing that than by taking a kid who feels left out and giving him a sense of belonging to a group that cares for him. The love of God

We have a dating system that glorifies the kids who are already glorified by our society and puts down the kids who are already put down.

makes us brothers and sisters, and an inclusive style for fun and recreation makes the feeling of "family" very real.

Youth ministers are constantly trying to work out what it means to be a Christian in the dating game. Because I stand back from the situation and observe rather than being involved like them in the nitty gritty of life, I can say this sociologically: Dating is a basically immoral institution.

Go to a high school dance and watch those kids who are sitting around on the chairs on the four sides, those girls that have that bored look of indifference as they try to conceal the hurt that comes from spending an evening rejected. I remember well one dance that I had to organize as senior class president at West Philadelphia High. At the end of the evening I was out on 48th street with some of my friends. Mary, my lab partner, came running out of the school. Neat girl, Mary. Witty, clever, and on top of all that, she was a ventriloquist. (It is dangerous sitting next to a witty ventriloquist in chemistry. Teacher says, "Gonna have a test tomorrow." I raise my hand. "What will it cover?" "Whatever is on my mind." And without moving her lips Mary says, "Then we don't have anything to worry about." And everybody breaks up. And then, after she's got me laughing, she looks at me with a How-could-you? look.)

But Mary just wasn't built right. After that dance she walks out, climbs into her car, and drives away. But before she can drive away I watch my friend Mary break down and cry. And I was angry with the system. Any system that could take my friend Mary and break her heart like that in a night is a system that is conceived by the demonic.

You get to any school dance and just watch the hurt pervading the place, and if you call this good, wholesome fun, you're a sick person. And what about those who stay home the night of the prom, and nobody wants to say the truth: "Janey, you're a reject." Any system that makes a kid feel like a reject you want to do battle with.

The time has come for Christians to look for alternatives to our present dating system. Christians ought to invent and promote a new style of dating.

When I was teaching at the University of Pennsylvania, I

became intrigued with a new style of dating that was emerging on the campus scene during the 1960s. They called it "group dating." Instead of boys and girls going off as pairs, a whole gang of kids would run around together. Nobody worried about who was linked with whom. All the kids simply had a good time together and enjoyed each other.

All it takes is for somebody to speak for the group and say, "Hey! Come on with us and have some fun. We're not practicing exclusive dating. Everybody can come along with us. We want everybody to share. Let's have a good time together. It won't be as much fun without you."

We have to condemn the whole dating system. Our responsibility is to run the kind of social activities where the group is built together as a cohesive unit rather than fragmented into paired-off couples. I think we've got to mock dating, ridicule it, declare war on it.

I'm not against kids falling in love, but they ought to fall in love after they get to know each other in a group, rather than in fact trying to date to find out who they are, because nothing's more phony than people that date. We need to come to know each other in depth before we end up in romantic relationships.

Turning Your Love Life Over to Jesus

There is a deeper kind of love than romance. It's the kind of love that grows up between two people who have the same goals and commitments in life. This kind of love goes much deeper.

What is that one thing that you will hold on to after you have sacrificed everything else? What is that for which you would die? Once you have defined what is so important that you are willing to sacrifice everything else, you ought to wait for somebody else who has the same commitment.

If you are a Christian, you are someone who says from the depths of your being, "For me to live is Christ, to die is gain." Consequently, you must marry someone who shares your commitment to Jesus. As each of you grows closer to Him you will simultaneously grow closer to each other.

That is why the Bible tells us, "Be not unequally yoked with nonbelievers." In the Old Testament, the Bible asks, "Can two walk together unless they be agreed?" For a love relationship to last over the long haul, it is essential that you both believe the same things about Christ. If the two of you are not committed to the same things, you will not be able to make a commitment to each other.

Jesus says, "Unless you love me more than you love your mother, your father, your sister, or your brother, you are not worthy of me." You can't be His follower unless you are into that.

A couple came to me to be married. The young woman had made a commitment to Christ in a Bible study group I had led. When I asked her fiancé if he was a Christian, he coolly announced he had once believed in God but had "grown out of that sort of thing."

I asked the young woman if she was going to marry him in spite of the fact that he wasn't a Christian. She angrily replied, "Don't go quoting the Bible to me, Campolo. You're always quoting the Bible."

I told her that she could not be a true Christian unless she loved Jesus more than she loved her fiancé, but she would not listen. However, something did get in the way of the two of them being together for the rest of their lives. They got divorced. I don't think a marriage can last if it's built upon the necessity of going against the known will of God.

There will be a signicant number of you who will not get married. Perhaps you may find yourself having to choose between marrying somebody who doesn't share your commitments, or not getting married at all. That is a hard choice to face, but I must tell you that there are a lot of things worse than being single the rest of your life. One of those is being married to someone with whom you do not have agreement in the things of God.

You may be asked to accept singleness if you follow Jesus. But nobody ever said that following Jesus would be easy. On the other hand, singleness can be a blessing. It can allow a person to serve Jesus in a way that is impossible for married people. The apostle Paul writes it in 1 Corinthians 7:32-34.

Show me a girl with a lousy self-image and I'll show you a female who is very easy to seduce sexually.

This requires that you order your sex life, marriage, or state of singleness in accord with His will. I am calling upon you to surrender your life to Jesus. If I were to ask you to give Him your money, I have a feeling that you might do that.

If I asked you to give some time to Him, most of you would do that, too. But I am asking for something deeper than that. I'm asking you to say from the depths of your heart, "I am going to let Jesus govern my life with members of the opposite sex. I am going to be sensitive to the kids who are hurting and left out. I am going to commit myself only to people who share my commitments to Him. I will accept singleness as an opportunity for greater service if He gives me the special grace to overcome my sexual longings."

Will you give your love life over to Jesus and trust Him that His way of doing things is the best way? I sure hope so. More than that, I pray so.

Dr. Anthony Campolo is an ordained Baptist minister and the chairman of the department of sociology at Eastern College in St. Davids, Pennsylvania. He's a popular speaker and the author of several books, including You Can Make a Difference, A Reasonable Faith, and *Partly Right.*

PURITY OF HEART can never be found in a religion or a theology. It is the person of Jesus Christ that accepts, loves, and purifies each one and places each one in His service.

—Heini Arnold

GOD WANTS SO VERY, VERY MUCH to give Himself to the poor, weak heart; but the heart must be absolutely open for God. Thus Jesus says in Matthew 6:22-24 that we live in darkness when we try to serve two masters. Purity of heart depends absolutely on giving oneself completely to Jesus. Without this complete surrender the eye is sick, and so the whole body is in darkness.

—Heini Arnold

PREGNANCY & ABORTION

ARE YOU UNMARRIED AND SEXUALLY ACTIVE? If you're an American teenager, chances are pretty good that you are. At least four out of ten young people in the U.S. between 14 and 19 have intercourse, and over one million girls become pregnant each year.

If you are involved in this, stop and think. *Stop and think.* You don't need to swallow everything TV tries to feed you about sex. Some people think that the only two options available to adolescents in our sex-crazed society are pregnancy or the Pill. But there is a third. And it's really the only sane, the only moral option. It's called continence, and it means saying *"No way."*

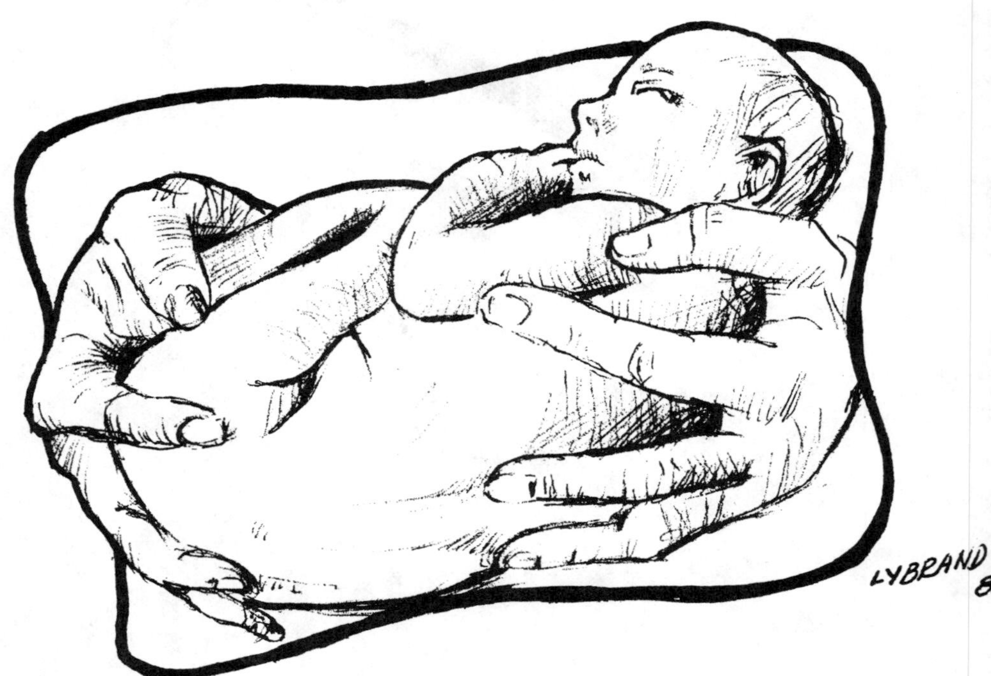

"TOO LATE—I'M ALREADY PREGNANT."

If you are pregnant and considering an abortion, or if you've gotten your girlfriend pregnant, read what Mother Teresa says in the next article. Think about it. There are agencies around the country that will help you through a pregnancy. One international organization devoted to providing positive alternatives to abortion is Birthright. Their central office is at 761 Coxwell Avenue, Toronto, Canada M4C 3C5, phone number: (416) 469-1111. They have centers all over the world. Just look up Birthright in the phone book. Another is Bethany Christian Services, a private, licensed child and family services agency committed to providing life alternatives for women who are pregnant. They provide family and pregnancy counseling, adoption and foster care services, residential treatment, and day care. Their corporate office is at 901 Eastern Avenue, N.E., Grand Rapids, MI 49503, (616) 459-6273. If you want help, try their Bethany Lifeline: 1-800-BETHANY. Or you could contact us. We'll do what we can. Write Hutterian Brethren, Rt. 213, Rifton, NY 12471 or call (914) 658-3141.

The people at these agencies love all three of you—father, mother, and baby. They know what you're going through. If you can't cope with raising a child, they'll help you find adoptive parents.

—the editors

PASCAL SAID, "You would not have sought me had you not already found me." These words help us to recognize, in humility, that Jesus loved us first. Each one who seeks a pure heart will always be drawn by God. This is a promise and he should hold on to it. God calls us through our conscience, and many times a person already carries Christ in his heart, even though he is not aware of it.

—Heini Arnold

Love for the Unborn Child

by Mother Teresa of Calcutta

LET US THANK GOD for giving us parents who wanted us, who loved us, and who helped us to grow. We who are parents or spiritual parents will make sure to show that tenderness and love for our little ones.

Even if a mother could forget her child, God says clearly, "I will not forget you. I have carved you on the palm of my hand. You are precious to me. I love you." Just think, God Himself declares his love for you, for me, for that little unborn child. He has created each one of us and all of those little ones in the womb of their mothers for great things—to love and to be loved.

A few weeks ago I had an extraordinary experience of the tenderness of God for the little one. A man came to our house. His only child was dying in the slums of Calcutta. He had a doctor's prescription for medicine that was not available in India. It had to be brought from England.

As we were talking, a man came with a basket of medicines. On top of the basket was the medicine we needed. I looked at the bottle. Millions and millions and millions of children in the world—how could God be concerned with this little child in the slums of Calcutta? See how precious this little one was to God?

God loves the unborn child as something very, very special. This is in the Gospel—"God loved the world so much that He gave His Son, Jesus." He came in the womb of a mother.

Today, that little unborn child is a target of destruction. Abortion destroys the beautiful image of God, the presence of God. For every unborn child is created in God's image. That is why abortion is such a terrible evil, a terrible destroyer of

If a mother can murder her child, what is left for others to do?

peace, love, unity, joy, and beauty.

Let us make one strong resolution: We will do everything to preserve life, not to destroy life. You and I must help the mothers, whoever they may be, wherever they may be. Let us help them to want the child. If they don't want him, tell them Mother Teresa and her sisters want him.

We are fighting abortion with adoption. Thousands of children have brought joy, peace, love, unity into families with no children. When we bring a child into a family, there is so much love. I've seen again and again the greatness of love.

Why are we allowing such evil everywhere—so much killing, so much destruction? I always give the same answer. If a mother can murder her child, what is left for others to do?

So, when you are thinking and talking—pray. Pray that

God will give you a clean heart to understand His love. Then you will be able to give that love to others. Jesus said, "Love one another as I have loved you." And to make it easy for us to love one another, He says, "Whatever you do for the least,

> Believe me, hunger is not only for a piece of bread, hunger is for love and being wanted.

you do for me." Help an unwed mother to get a good home; help her to be loved, to feel that someone wants her. You can help her child to be wanted, to be loved, to be tenderly cared for. Give that love. Don't be afraid. Share that love; share until it hurts.

Have you experienced the joy of loving? True love hurts. It hurt Jesus to love us and it hurt God to have to give Jesus to die for us. Do not be afraid to love until it hurts, because Jesus has made it very clear—if in my name you receive the little unborn child, you receive me.

But when you are talking of a life of love, of compassion, ask your own heart, *is my family all right?* Love begins there.

Pray first with your own family. If you pray together, you will learn how to love each other as God loves you. We have so many young people in the streets everywhere, in all the cities. Why are they—school children—in the streets? No one is in the house to receive them. Be at home to love one another, love father, mother, children. Love begins at home.

Jesus came all the way from heaven. He came as a little child to teach us how to love from the beginning. He could have come like a big man. He could have been somebody special. But no, He came like a little, helpless child to give us the good news that God loves us, that God is love and He loves you and He loves me.

Let us also understand the terrible poverty and fear of the

mother of the unborn child—one more child to feed, one more to educate. What is strange is that I have never seen this fear among our poor people as I have seen it in people that are better off and can afford to have children.

The little unborn child is the poorest, most unwanted, uncared for, rejected of the poor.

I will never forget the poor leper woman, so badly disfigured. What tenderness was in her heart for her little child. But as soon as the baby was born, we had to take him before the mother had even kissed him. The mother looked with tears rolling down her face. I thought of the millions of children who are killed by their mothers. This poor woman had such tenderness. What a sacrifice she made not to kiss her child so that the child would remain healthy. For that little one, Jesus died on the cross.

Believe me, hunger is not only for a piece of bread, hunger is for love and being wanted. We take a special vow to give wholehearted service to the poorest of the poor. The little unborn child is the poorest, most unwanted, uncared for, rejected of the poor. Unborn children are worse off than lepers, much worse.

Let us pray that the tenderness and love of God can penetrate our hearts and we may help the unborn child to come, to be loved and wanted.

FAITH IN THE MYSTERY OF GOD'S GRACE can be the beginning of the healing process. Trust in Jesus and the unburdening of our heart in this trust can lead to such a healing that our whole being is poured out before God.

—Heini Arnold

DEPRESSION & SUICIDE

GOD ALONE knows what goes on in the heart of a man. I doubt if a man can say that even he himself knows what goes on in his own heart. . . . I believe that God sees deeper into the person's heart and sees the real will, which does not want these evil thoughts, pictures, or images. Some people think they are the only ones who are tormented by such things and therefore don't dare to speak about them.

—Heini Arnold

The Statistics

SUICIDE STATISTICS are hard to pin down. The experts offer a broad range of estimates. One of the problems is that many deaths officially recorded as accidents are more probably suicides. The death of a teenager driving south on the north-bound freeway at night with no headlights is, obviously, not the "accident" it's recorded as. But there's insurance coverage on accidents. And there's a stigma on a suicide in the family.

But a conservative estimate tells us that 30,000 Americans will take their own lives this year, though the American Association of Suicidology believes the more accurate figure to be 100,000. *100,000 human lives.* Of these, between 5,000 and 7,000 will be young people between 15 and 24. That makes suicide at least the third, possibly the second, leading cause of death among teenagers. (Accidents account for most adolescent deaths. Homicide or suicide, depending on whose figures you use, ranks second.) But for every teenager that succeeds, between 50 and 100 will attempt. Girls will attempt three times more frequently than boys; boys succeed four times as often as girls.

To compound this tragedy, the last few years have seen a frequent occurrence of the "cluster" phenomenon. It seems that suicide among young people may be in some way contagious: four suicides in four weeks among the classmates of the New Trier West High School outside Chicago; five in New York's affluent, suburban Westchester County in 20 days; five in Columbus, Ohio, in one month; six in the Dallas suburb of Plano in six months.

Adolescent suicide has tripled in the last two to three decades. The causes of this profoundly disturbing trend has been the subject of numerous articles and books. People are becoming concerned. But much more needs to be done. No one can hide from the grim facts. Your classmate, your friend, your sister, your son, might be next.

There Is Help Out There

by Carol Greenberg Felsenthal

SINCE HER FATHER'S DEATH in a car crash the year before, Sue Blake, 17, had become so shy that she ate lunch alone every day. "I thought I had nothing to live for," she says. "When Dad died, I lost my best friend. And Mom ignored me."

Sue also lost her self-confidence. She was convinced her father had committed suicide: "If Dad could abandon me, I figured I wasn't worth sticking around for."

She fantasized incessantly about killing herself, until one day, she tried to turn fantasy into reality. She swallowed sleeping pills.

"I panicked," she recalls. "I prayed I hadn't taken enough to kill me. The nausea was awful. I had this urge to explain why I did it. I called the operator, who connected me with

Evanston Hospital's Crisis Intervention Center. 'Well, I guess I'll just die now,' I told Jerry, the psychologist who answered. He screamed, 'Hey, wait! Don't hang up.' He seemed to really care. All of a sudden I was screaming, 'I don't want to die!' Then he said, 'I don't want you to die, either.' And I believed him.

"He sent someone to get me and was at the hospital when I arrived. My mom was there too—more upset, I thought, about her spoiled evening than about me.

"I still see Jerry regularly. And things still aren't great with my mom. But I've learned that if I don't start dealing with my problems, I'll end up unhappy like my mom—or worse yet, like my dad."

"MY MOTHER HAS ALWAYS THOUGHT my two older brothers were perfect," says 16-year-old Marilyn Jacobsen. "I mean, to her, they're a combination of Robert Redford and Albert Einstein.

"It wouldn't have been so bad if she hadn't been so disappointed in me. She'd be playing bridge, and a neighbor would be bragging about her daughter's going to the country club dance with Dr. So-and-so's son. My mom would come home and be disgusted with me because I haven't had a real date in my whole life. Then when grades came out, she was really furious because—as she put it—I wasn't 'Harvard material.'

"I decided to kill myself when girls started getting asked to the junior prom. I couldn't bear the thought of spending prom night with my scowling mother. Instead, I spent it with her in the emergency room, with tubes sticking out of my nose. I was thinking, 'Boy, you can't do anything right. You're even a flop at killing yourself.'

"Then a counselor walked in, sat down with her feet up on my bed, and said loudly, 'The doc called me and said you tried to kill yourself. Why?' What a relief! Before she came in, there was so much tension because everyone was trying to act like nothing happened.

"After that, I talked with her at a nearby drop-in center a couple of times a week. Now I'm spending my spare time there playing backgammon or just hanging around—which sure beats sulking in my room. I'm even starting to understand Mom better."

SUE AND MARILYN (their names have been changed) are two

very different teenagers with one identical, all-too-common, all-too-often-fatal belief that a brush with death will bring them the love, attention, and respect they are desperate for in life. Their suicide attempts were what psychiatrists call "cries for help." Neither Sue nor Marilyn really wanted to die. Both wanted caring, understanding, and someone to tell them, "I value you. You are a worthwhile person."

Neither realized that the help they needed was nearby. They didn't understand that, at the very least, the physical pain and mental anguish caused by the suicide attempt itself could have been avoided if they—or their friends—had known where to go and whom to turn to for help.

Sue and Marilyn are lucky. They didn't die, and they got the help they needed. But each could easily have become a statistic, one of the thousands of teens who each year cause their own death. Or counselors might not have been alerted, and the girls, unaided, might have tried suicide again—not being lucky enough to survive the second time. Of every five people who commit suicide, four have made previous attempts—presumably pleas that went unheeded. "The terrible tragedy," says Dr. Mary Giffin, a North Shore psychiatrist who treats depressed teenagers, "is that most of those who commit suicide are desperate for help and don't know how to find it."

Here, then, are the stories of five similarly desperate teens who *did* figure out how to get help with their problems before it was too late.

- Amy was caught shoplifting: "After that, my mom had so little trust in me that she wouldn't let me out of her sight, except to go to school."

  Instead of facing her problems and her parents, Amy ran away from them—to nearby Chicago. She soon exhausted her money, energy, self-respect—and the desire to live. After her second suicide attempt, she called her suburb's police department and asked if there was an agency in the suburb that helped runaways. There was. The policeman gave Amy the number of the agency's director—a young social worker named Linda. Linda drove down to the city and took Amy out to dinner, then home to her parents. During the next month, Linda met frequently with Amy and her mother and father. Together, they worked out a plan in which Amy would regain privileges in exchange for her passing her courses and following rules—rules that Amy and her parents set together.

- Jimmie cast himself in the role of class clown. "Everybody thinks I'm a real riot," he says. "I get invited to all the parties—but no one takes me seriously. And now that we're juniors, all anyone talks about is college boards. I've spent so much time goofing off, I can barely read."

  Jimmie jumped from his school's third-floor landing, leaving his pals laughing and himself in stitches—33 of them. He knew he was suicidal and that he'd better get help quick. He ruled out the school counseling department because he knew that after his second visit his parents would be informed. (Most high school counselors are required to notify parents after a teen's second or third visit.) But he did ask the counselor where he could get free psychiatric aid. The counselor made an appointment for Jimmie with a psychologist at the county mental health clinic. (In most areas, there are mental health clinics that charge patients according to their ability to pay.) The counselor explained to Jimmie that Illinois is one of the many states where a minor over 14 can get therapy without his parent's permission.

  Jimmie has been seeing the psychologist, Mr. Cummings, for nearly nine months now. With Mr. Cummings' help, he enrolled in a tutoring program at the public library. He's also applying to several out-of-state colleges. "I agree with Mr. Cummings that college is my best chance to start fresh," Jimmie says. "I want to go where nobody knows me; where I can just be a person instead of a bad imitation of Steve Martin."

- Fran moved to the North Shore in her sophomore year because her parents wanted her to go to the progressive New Trier Public High School. They couldn't really afford to live in the area so they rented an apartment in one of the suburb's few apartment buildings. "It's tough enough to break into these cliques when you've got the right clothes," Fran says. "It's impossible when you live in the same building as everyone else's maid."

"I couldn't bear the thought of spending prom night with my scowling mother. Instead, I spent it with her in the emergency room, with tubes sticking out of my nose."

Fran started getting sick nearly every weekday morning—so sick she couldn't go to school. Her parents insisted she see the school counselor. She refused, saying, "No one connected with that place could possibly help me." Meanwhile, she read in the newspaper an interview with a counselor named Kim from her town's drop-in center.

"This is a great place for kids who feel alienated from school, who aren't in the 'in' crowd," Kim says. "Many of our regulars start coming for counseling only. Before long, they're coming to play pool, to listen to music, to see their friends." Fran made an appointment to see Kim the next day after school.

Fran continued seeing Kim twice a week but always

dashed to the door right after her appointment. She was afraid of being snubbed—and hurt—again. But when Kim asked her to help with plans to raise money for the center, Fran couldn't refuse. Within a week, she was at the center nearly every day, working with her committee. "It sounds funny to call them my committee," she says. "I mean, a couple of them have turned into my friends."

- Joanne was convinced her parents didn't care about her. "They're both college professors, and they must have read somewhere that adolescents should have complete freedom—or maybe they just don't want the hassle of raising a kid. My friends are all into drugs, and I'm getting pushed that way too. We were smoking pot in the living room, and my dad walked right by and went into his study. He didn't say a word."

  Joanne approached Tom, whom she had seen talking to other kids in the lunchroom and parking lot. She knew he was an outreach worker—there to help people like herself who didn't know who else to turn to. "I could tell he was really happy to talk to me," Joanne recalls.

  With Joanne's permission, Tom spoke with her parents, explaining that they were giving their daughter everything but the attention and direction she craved. "They took him seriously," Joanne says, "I guess, because he's an adult and he has a couple of degrees. When I went out last night, my mom actually asked where I was going—and listened when I told her."

- Mike had everything—or so people thought. He was a good athlete, a top student, a natural leader—president of the student council. But Mike felt differently: "I'm empty. My parents are filled with pride, and I'm empty. I don't know what it all means."

  Mike suddenly stopped studying. When he turned in a

theme—two weeks late—about a valedictorian who hangs himself on graduation day, his English teacher stopped him after class. "I deliberately chose to send my SOS to Mr. Collins," Mike explains. "He really cares about kids. I knew he'd respond."

They talked for a long time that day and met periodically over the next few months. "Mike needed to know that people would still like him even if he didn't get good grades and make touchdowns," Mr. Collins says. "He also, for once in his life, needed to do something just for fun, something he wouldn't be graded on. I'm a photography buff, and I got Mike interested in that. He'll never be a Richard Avedon, but that's one of the reasons he enjoys it so much."

Carol Greenberg Felsenthal's articles have appeared in a variety of national magazines. She is currently working on her third book, a biography of Alice Rosa Longworth, to be published by Putnam in September 1987. She lives in Chicago.

SUICIDE IS NOT A NORMAL DEATH. It is tragic beyond the most shattering experiences. There is something about suicide that, even when done as an escape from an agonizing terminal illness, signals complete and utter defeat. It is without any semblance of nobility or pride.

No matter how bad the pain is, it's never so bad that suicide is the only answer. It's never so bad that the only escape is a false one. Suicide doesn't end pain. It only lays it on the broken shoulders of the survivors.

—Anne-Grace Scheinin

Anne-Grace Scheinin has lived through severe bouts of depression, several adolescent attempts at suicide, and her own mother's suicide in 1976.

Suicide Is No Answer

EVERY YEAR we lose several young people in our community to suicide. We keep hoping it will stop, but so far it hasn't. I hear it is a national epidemic. Once every 90 minutes a teenager in this country commits suicide. This is for every youth who is considering ending it all:

You haven't seen the world that exists outside your family. Soon you will be on your own and then you will understand what is important and what is not important.

What you don't know is that 15 minutes after you decide to kill yourself, you might have felt better. Or two hours later, or two days, or two years.

What you don't know is that you are stronger than you think. You can find another girlfriend, or you can stand being shamed more than you realize. Failing in school, getting in trouble with the law may be painful, but you can get over it. You can fix it. Don't be killing yourself over events that you may barely remember 10 years from now.

What you don't know is that there is nothing romantic or mysterious or "deep" about killing yourself. It is an awful mess that you can never understand until you have kids of your own.

What you don't know is that suicide is sneaky and spiteful and filled with anger. If you are thinking about suicide, you are furious with somebody. You can be furious without killing yourself or thinking you need the punishment of death.

What you also don't know is that suicide is forever, and nobody, not your parents or your doctor, can fix it. You won't be around for the funeral. And you won't be coming back.

So get smart. Go to California. Find a therapist. Lapse into sadness. Become mad as the dickens. Do your time in jail. But get off the suicide kick. It's a dead end.

—Tom Heisler

This piece appeared originally as a letter to the editor in the Arkansas Gazette. *Tom lives in Wynne, Arkansas.*

The Warning Signs

SUICIDE, says writer David Breskin, is "but the period at the end of a long sentence that no one's read." It has been called the ultimate act of communication. In other words, teenagers contemplating suicide often give signals of their intent. Watch for these:

- Talk of suicide
- Previous attempts
- Personality changes: withdrawal, aggression, promiscuity, substance abuse, depression, apathy
- Changes in eating or sleeping habits
- Drop in school performance
- Themes of death or depression in essays or artwork
- Loss of friend, especially through suicide
- Making final arrangements: giving away prized possessions; writing a will
- Pregnancy

What To Do

If You Think Someone Might Be Suicidal

- *Listen.* And take everything he says seriously. Let him know you want to help.
- Ask directly if he has considered suicide: "Do you ever wake up in the morning and wish you hadn't? Do you ever feel like ending it all—like killing yourself?" Ask if he has a plan (how, when, where). The more detailed the plan, the more serious the threat.
- Be affirmative and supportive. Let him know you'll do everything you can to pull him through.
- Ask for help: school counselor, minister, psychiatrist (see box "Where to find help"). Get the family involved.
- Remove any guns, potentially lethal drugs, and alcohol from his reach.
- Stay with him if there is any indication that he will carry through with his threat.

THE DEVIL IS A REALITY ***and tries to attack each person at his weakest point, each religious group at its weakest point, and even every nation at its weakest point.***

—Heini Arnold

What Matters Is that Someone Cares

by Karen Peters,
Ulster County (NY) Family Court Judge

SUICIDE IS THE ULTIMATE DESPERATE ACT any human being can commit, and it is the most tragic death that occurs in our society. It is tragic because it is preventable: the primary cause of death among males in this country between the ages of 16 and 24 is alcohol-related crashes; the two secondary causes are suicide and homicide. That means that the two major causes of death of young males in our country are preventable by some education, some love, some concern, some communication. Why then the 300% increase in suicide since the '60s?

I wonder how many of our children have positive role models in the home and in their community. How can they?

They see their parents' relationship crumble and collapse in divorce and then hear their parents fight heatedly over their custody. Do these children have a member of the extended family they can turn to for support? Not usually. We're so mobile in modern America that these children don't have a grandparent, aunt, or uncle nearby who can fill in for their distracted parents.

We adults have a tendency to downplay what to a child is a critical issue. I would only hope that each of us, when a child confronts us, would remember this rule: Whatever a child thinks is a crisis *is* a crisis for them, and they need the attention of an adult who loves them.

Not only have we had an enormous increase in suicide in this country in recent years, but in Ulster County, New York, in the past two years we have had a 600% increase in parents charged with abuse and neglect of their own children. The situation is of crisis proportions, and it is not something that we can continue to ignore.

When I see parents in my court telling me their kids don't listen to them, I am reminded of a maxim that happens to be embedded in our legal code. It says, "By listening to more than mere words, I can learn much more than mere words." Judges and lawyers call this "demeanor." We try to discern the demeanor of the person in front of us as well as what they say. How do they hold their body? How do they gesture? Do they appear happy, sad, tense, confused, disordered? I

We adults have a tendency to downplay what to a child is a critical issue.

firmly believe that we adults often fail to pick up such signals from the children we see every day. And, most serious of all, we fail to really listen to what those children have to say to us. Communicating with persons, truly communicating, requires respecting them as human beings, respecting their feelings and believing those feelings deserve our attention. We tend to be impatient. We move with enormous speed. And because of that we often fail to give time and attention to our youth who will some day take the reins of power from us.

It has been said that most people don't ever consider suicide. But I have. When I was 13 I was very lucky to have a mother and father. I had a very good talking relationship with my father. I wasn't aware then how much it meant. I didn't get along very well with my mother. One day when I came home from school I was told that my father had gone off to work and dropped dead. No one had had any indication that he would go.

The next year of my life was very, very difficult. There was no one I could talk to, no one I trusted, no one I felt could really listen to me or really cared about me. And at that time in my life I did consider suicide.

Somehow I survived that time without anybody to turn to. I didn't commit that desperate act. I believe that each of us during our childhood has had some terrible experience to confront, and confronting such an experience is always a lot easier when there's somebody we can trust who will hold us—or if we need hugging, hug us—and listen to our struggles and our fears. Whether our fears are real or imagined doesn't matter. What matters is that someone cares.

Karen Peters is serving a ten-year term as judge of the Ulster County, New York, Family Court. Previously she served as Counsel to the New York State Division for Alcoholism and Alcohol Abuse. Judge Peters lives in Rosendale, New York.

Schools Must Help Prevent These Tragedies

by Pamela Cantor

IT'S 1:30 P.M. The principal has been notified that one of his students has been found in a car in the school parking lot. He shot himself, apparently during his lunch break. What should the principal do?

This nightmare could bring suicide attempts and suicides by other students. This happened in Texas, Pennsylvania, Nebraska, and New York.

The principal should not wait. By the time he hears the details, the rest of the school will have heard the details, too, in 40 different versions.

The principal must notify the parents. Then he should call a school-wide assembly and explain as much as he knows. If students are let out without any explanations, they will make up their own.

He should designate staff students can turn to. He should have mental health professionals there to answer questions. Ideally, teachers would already have information about suicide and depression.

That evening, he should hold a community meeting for all parents and students. This will give the parents information. It will let the teenagers have a forum for their concerns and a place to go rather than hanging out and escalating the hysteria these situations often provoke.

The mental health professionals should be in school all day, every day, for the next three weeks. They should speak to all close friends and classmates of the boy who committed suicide. They should target and support any who have recently experienced a loss, particularly one by death.

A boy tragically made the wrong choice. This calls for sorrow, not honor.

The principal should *not* call off school so everyone can attend the funeral. Kids need to express their grief; they do not need to romanticize a mistake.

A boy tragically made the wrong choice. This calls for sorrow, not honor. We should not make a youngster who made a poor choice into a hero. Instead, we should applaud the wisdom of those who choose to start psychotherapy and take constructive action to deal with their concerns.

I fear that a troubled child, struggling to find an identity and to feel important, may grasp at this negative model as a way of gaining much-wanted notoriety. He may not understand that, after death, he won't enjoy the popularity.

Pamela Cantor is a clinical psychologist and the president of the American Association of Suicidology.

Where to Find Help

Crisis Intervention Centers

There are over 500 centers across the country where you can call for help 24 hours a day, seven days a week. To find the center nearest you:

- Look in the front of your phone book in the "Community Service Numbers" section or in the Yellow Pages under "Suicide."
- Call the American Association of Suicidology at (303) 692-0985 or write AAS, 2459 S. Ash St., Denver, CO 80222. They can refer you to someone who can help. They also keep an up-to-date listing of every suicide prevention and crisis intervention agency in the U.S.
- Look under "CONTACT" in the phone book (there are 90 CONTACT centers across the U.S.). If there is nothing listed, write or phone their central office at CONTACT USA, Pouch A, Harrisburg, PA 17105, (717) 232-3501 and they can refer you to the agency nearest you.
- Call the National Save-A-Life League in New York City at (718) 492-4668 or the Suicide Prevention Center of Los Angeles at (213) 386-5111.

Hospitals

Call your community hospital and ask for the intake worker in psychiatry. If the patient has already attempted suicide, call an ambulance.

Other sources

To find out what's available in your community (drop-in centers, mental health clinics, hospitals with crisis-intervention units), call:

- School counseling department.
- Public relations department of your city hall.
- Education reporter for your local newspaper.
- Reference librarian at your public library.

Also check under "Mental Health" or "Clinics" in the Yellow Pages.

THOUGHTS ARE GIANTS. If evil thoughts are deliberate—*be they of power over other people as Hitler represented in Germany or be they of impurity, hatred, or any other such evil—then we will act like that some day.*

—Heini Arnold

CRIME

LYBRAND
-86

The Better Way
A Testimony

by Walter Wilson

I GREW UP IN HARLEM on the streets of crime. My first arrest came when I was nine years old. I didn't know what the word "burglary" meant. I did know that that's what they said I was arrested for and I knew I had stolen things. They let me go because of my age.

Poor, black, a man—three strikes against me, three shames, three curses, driving me toward a lifestyle all too normal in Harlem. At 16, after numerous run-ins with the law and arrests, I was streetwise and at war with the establishment. My overriding concern was to perfect my strategy, learn from my mistakes, and beat the system.

In Harlem your 16th birthday marks the day you become, in the eyes of the law, criminally adult—that is, you are punished for your crimes with adult punishment. So I made the usual adjustments in crime style, replacing robbery and burglary with petty theft and gambling. Trouble was, someone got me hooked on heroin, and by the time I was 18 I couldn't afford a low criminal profile. The expenses of the heroin habit "necessitated" a four-year crime spree that ended in nine arrests and four prison sentences.

Between the ages of 18 and 22, the only periods of clear-headedness were those in prison or jail. These interludes prevented my total enslavement to drugs. Now I see in those sentences the hand of God—but then I saw them as times to groom my crime strategy, never as a time to consider a change of heart.

By the time I was 21 I had firmly decided that in place of abusing myself with drugs, I'd sell them to other people so they could abuse themselves. In Harlem you either peddle drugs or rob people or run numbers. Some try work at regular jobs, but few can take the steady erosion of self-respect that goes along with these jobs.

For the next nine years I sold drugs literally every day I was out of prison in the streets. I called this "being free from heroin." I didn't want to admit that heroin was in firm control of my life in a more subtle way.

During these years I taught myself enough law to argue my own cases, occasionally to beat my own raps and, at the least, to get substantial reductions in my sentences. My courtroom antics won me a grand reputation among criminals, for I had "matched wits" with real lawyers and won several times. It was exhilarating. I had potential. I had "class." I could become truly wealthy as a titled career criminal. Such were my prison reflections in 1977.

When I hit the streets again that year, I quickly used my underworld contacts to get myself established as a shooting gallery proprieter—one of those places where dope fiends come, pay their money, rent a needle, buy drugs, and get high. When they finish, you put them out on the street to make room for the next customers.

Money poured in, but it didn't do me a bit of good. I squandered it all on clothes, cars, and an unfortunate taste I had developed—cocaine. After three years of uninterrupted freedom, the emptiness of my life hit me. Wealth and status did not add up to a life worth living. I distrusted my fellow man and was subject to waves of severe depression. I was lost and I knew it. Inwardly I began to ask God for an answer.

About this time the "worst" happened. The police raided my spot, tore it to pieces, and hauled everyone in sight off to jail. As usual I had escaped their net. When the heat was off, I crept back to the gallery to survey the damage. Rubbish and rubble everywhere. But what's that? Of all things, in the midst of the mess lay a Bible. In my despair I picked it up and decided to read it straight through to find out for myself what was really behind all this talk about there being something else in life—God, Jesus, religion, and what have you.

It took me about a year to get through the Bible, from page one to the end. Here I was, a 30-year-old black male criminal. What could I expect to find in any life, in any book? And yet God began to speak to me as I turned those pages. God exists and He wants me to ask Him what I should do with my life. He tells me to quit the drug business and, through the passage in Luke that says you should put your energies into looking for the Kingdom and let God take care of the rest, He gave me the faith to do it.

For two more years I hibernated with my Bible, and after that I said, "All right, Lord, I'm ready. Send me out into the streets." And the first person I ran into was Joseph Holland who invited me to a Bible study with the members of Harlem's Ark of Freedom, or HARK. I went.

In this group I found a Christian community with a Bible-based vision to uplift our aching Harlem community—a vision right from the heart. I knew then that I was a part of them.

I began working with HARK in every detail. I was blessed in ways that were inconceivable. I completed a course in housing management, another in insurance. I began working with my 5000 fellow tenants in our housing project. Somehow the Lord had gotten me involved in a movement that aspires to turn all of Harlem around.

Today, three years later, I am a resident member of HARK, employed and active in Christian counseling. I credit the power of God for these accomplishments.

Jesus is the better way. The other way is death and destruction.

WE CAN PUT A GOOD THOUGHT, a prayer, our love to God into our hearts "on purpose," and it will be in us and live in us and work in us until sometime or other it appears again in the conscious life. This is also true if we give room in ourselves to an evil thought or an evil image. This thought or image is often concealed for a long time; suddenly it is there, and the effect that it had and has on our inner life is also suddenly there.

—Heini Arnold

HOMOSEXUALITY

There are so many people living the gay life—can they all be wrong? If so many are doing it, does that mean it's O.K.? What about sexual orientation? Is that just another life-style? Or is it your personal makeup? Or both? Is there a right and a wrong, or is it all up to you and what you like?

You don't hear much anymore about "commitment" or a "life calling." Now it's "life-style" or "personal choice" or "what's in it for me?"

The following article is by a man who was once a practicing homosexual. But he thought about it and started to care about right and wrong. He sacrificed his homosexual life for a much greater thing—following Jesus.

He deserves our respect now just as he needed our love before his decision. Jesus always loved a person most when he had to reject what that person was doing—with his life or his sexuality. And the practice of homosexuality is something we must reject; the Bible speaks too clearly against it.

Sex and sexuality, whether homo- or heterosexually oriented, must be firmly in God's hands. No one should enter even a heterosexual relationship without God's express blessing through marriage. And it may be that God's plan for you does not include marriage. Then these demands will be hard and will call for pain and self-denial. But they are possible. They are possible for those who have found the meaning of Jesus' paradox: "He who loses his life for my sake will find it."

—the editors

The Challenge of a Changed Life

by Ed Hurst

WHEN I WAS TWO, they tell me that I broke a baby bottle over my younger brother's head. I must have felt he was getting all the attention, and I wanted more of it for me. Greed for more attention and jealousy over what he was getting prompted my attack. Probably around age three I had a first-hand experience with slander. While playing with a ball in the livingroom, I knocked over a lamp. When my mom asked who did it, I blamed it on another brother who had just gone out the door.

The following year, at Halloween, I learned to steal and swindle. As we dumped our bags of Halloween goodies on the floor, my eyes saw "treasures" in the piles my other brothers had, and I got quite good at swindling the younger ones. "I'll trade you two of these shiny Hershey's Kisses for that one plain candy bar," I said . . . fully aware that the candy bar was worth at least twice as much. What I couldn't get by trading, I sometimes got by stealing. When a bag was left unguarded, I would "snitch" the treasure I desired.

When I got caught there was always a price to pay. When I pleaded that "I just couldn't help it," my parents sat me down and explained that I could. They knew it wasn't easy. They

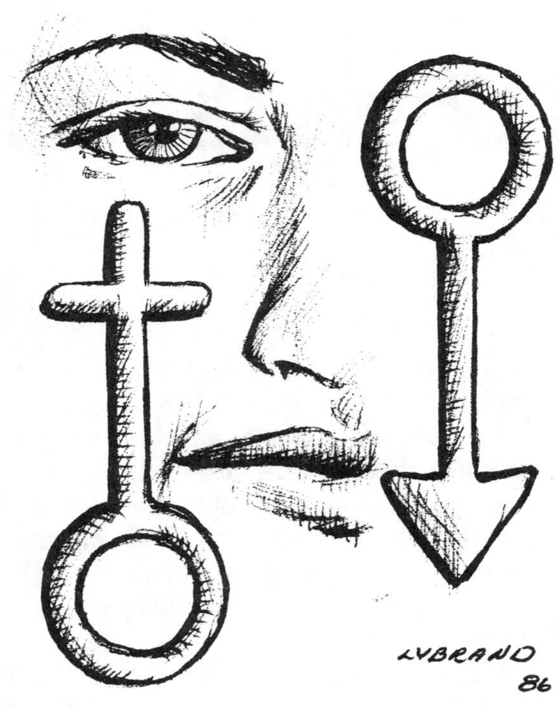

knew that the sin nature was at work in me but that the sinful desire had to be overcome. As a result of their good parenting, I have control in those areas now. I'm still tempted, of course. Greed is still with me; so is jealousy. I still look for others to blame and, when I'm angry with someone, I am likely to at least *want* to say bad things about them. Stealing isn't a major problem at all but swindling can be . . . particularly around tax time. There are things I don't want to report. Eventually, though, I always do.

FROM THIS EVIDENCE it would seem that I was born greedy. I was born jealous. I'm a born swindler, slanderer, and thief. No one taught me how; the desires—and the abilities to carry them about—simply sprang up within me. Both the desires and the abilities remain with me to this day. I have been thankful for parents, friends, pastors, and teachers who have taught me that these desires are either sinful or nonproductive. Without their counsel and encouragement, I am sure that I would struggle far more severely today.

Those aren't the only sins I struggled with. Paul, in his letter to the Corinthians, lists the type of people who will not inherit the kingdom of God: the sexually immoral, idolators, adulterers, male prostitutes, homosexual offenders, thieves, the greedy, drunkards, slanderers, and swindlers. I struggled with many of these sins. When I reached adolescence, I had a burning curiosity for any type of pornography. By the time I reached college, I also had my first experiences with drugs and drunkenness. My main problem, however, was with one of the least "popular" sins on the list.

As the middle son of seven sons, I stuck out like the proverbial sore thumb. In a small town given to athletics, I lacked in both abilities and interest. I was not like the other boys and never had been. When puberty hit, I realized that I was more fascinated by the boys than by the girls. Suddenly, everything began to make sense. From the time I was eleven, I knew that I was homosexual.

Regarding this issue, I began receiving some contradictory messages. Some people were calling it a tragedy and a sickness; some were calling it the "sickest sin there was." Others were declaring, however, that it wasn't wrong at all . . . that it was natural . . . that I was simply "born that way." I wrestled between the two, and eventually the latter began to make the most sense. After all I *had* been different *all* my life.

Although I tried to keep it a secret, rumors began to spread. Some assumed I was gay because I was different; some assumed it because of my looks and the way I dressed; some assumed it by the people I hung out with. By the time I reached my second year in college, it was no longer a secret at all. Not only was I not secretive but I also began publicly spreading the news in a sincere desire to end the oppression of gays. Several years later, I had a personal encounter with the Lord.

My encounter was not an easy one. I had spent a lifetime coming to grips with my homosexuality and now I was being told that homosexual behavior was a sin. It felt as if my entire being, my whole identity, was being challenged. Yet it seemed right somehow to trust my Creator with my life. I also began to see that there was something in between those two messages I had been hearing. While the Bible was calling homosexuality a sin, it wasn't calling it the "sickest sin" or a "tragic illness" . . . it was simply calling it a sin like any other sin. What's more, the Bible offered hope! 1 Corinthians 6:11, after listing all of the sins I've been discussing here, said "And such *were* some of you. . . ." This was something worth exploring.

FOR THE PAST 12 YEARS I've been doing just that . . . The more I explore, the more I realize how wrong I was to conclude that God somehow "made me gay" and desired for me to stay that way. God, it seems, can only be credited with making me "unique"; it is society's inability to accept that "uniqueness" that created my homosexual problems.

My parents relate that the childrearing that they had learned did not prepare them for me. I was more sensitive, easily hurt, defensive, and withdrawn. I preferred books to sports. I was very private and independent. These same qualities did little to endear me to my brothers or to the kids at school. These qualities weren't "wrong"; there wasn't anything sexual about them; they were simply "different." But because my uniqueness was treated as a problem and because it was not affirmed as something good, I began to think that there was something wrong with being different.

My parents loved me but I tended to remember the times they failed me rather than the times when they showed their love and support. My brothers loved me, too, but there were many times when our differences created major problems. I did not relish their athletic accomplishments since I viewed these as areas where they were "better than me"; they did not relish my academic accomplishments for the same reason. It seems we always only saw the differences; in these past 12 years I have marvelled at how much we really are alike.

I can see now that my lust for men was most often a desire to be accepted and loved. The men I pursued were men who represented what I wished I could be. Because these were feelings and because there was a strong element of attraction (I admired these men) and desire (they possessed qualities that I wanted), I mistook the longings for sexual ones.

TODAY, I STILL HAVE DESIRES; I still have wants and needs. Many of these are directed towards other men. But, when I'm faced with temptation, I now ask myself, "What is it that you're *really* wanting? Is it sex or acceptance? Is it a desire to have sex or simply to be loved? Do you want to have sex with him or do you simply want to be like him?" The answers expose the real problem; they also expose my real need.

Neither the problem nor the need can be denied. Hiding from them will not make them go away. Attempting to resolve them through homosexual experience will not resolve them. Meeting these needs in legitimate ways is possible, yet extremely difficult. Our society—and our churches—offer few avenues where healthy nonsexual, same-gender friendships can be cultivated.

The needs for genuine love, acceptance, and affirmation are not met in the 60-second "hug thy neighbor" portion of the church service. They are not met at a "fellowship meal" where dozens of near strangers are told to get acquainted. Quite often, they are not even met in a "home fellowship" setting. The fears and insecurities of a lifetime are not easily shared with a group. There is a need for some one-to-one fellowship. One-to-one fellowship frequently demands more time and personal commitment than most of us are willing or able to give. Largely for this reason, those who struggle with homosexuality in our churches continue to struggle . . . their real needs are being left unmet.

THOSE WHO ARE HOMOSEXUAL do not need to be affirmed in their homosexuality. While I can commend the compassion that would support such affirmation, I cannot commend the affirmation itself. We can express love and support for an individual without condoning sinful behavior. In recent years, we have learned this principle as it applies to other life-dominating problems. We do not cast the alcoholics from our churches; instead, we offer the support and counsel that helps them to overcome their problem. This is the type of compassion that we should be offering to the homosexual.

This type of commitment and compassion goes beyond what we normally express. It even transcends the compassion that says "they've suffered enough; we shouldn't add to their problems by calling it sin." Real love gets involved. It challenges; it confronts; it corrects. It also supports and strengthens. It accepts you "where you're at" while it challenges you to be a better person tomorrow.

For this reason, the homosexual issue does not need to destroy or "infect" the Church, as so many fear it will do. Instead, this issue will challenge and provoke the Church to express a love that runs deeper and a commitment that lasts longer. We do not need to fear the issue nor do we need to fear those individuals who struggle with it personally. In many ways, "they" are "us." Think back to those "more common" sins I mentioned earlier. The homosexual sin was in the middle of the same list! The wages for *all* sin is death. The remedy for *all* sin is the sacrifice of Jesus Christ. With this in mind, we share a lot in common with every sinner—regardless of his sin. May that knowledge humble us and build a heart of true compassion within us.

IF WE WANT TO BE HEALED of the wounds made by Satan's tricks and arrows—by evil feelings, thoughts, or ideas—we must have absolute trust in Jesus so that even if we feel nothing yet, we give ourselves absolutely and without reserve to Jesus with all we are and have. Ultimately, all we have is our sin. We must lay our sin before Him in trust. Then He will give us forgiveness, cleansing, and peace of heart; and these lead to a love that cannot be described.

It is said very clearly in the New Testament that forgiveness of sin is connected with the Church. . . . Forgiveness is not merely a private matter; it is closely connected with the Church. Repentance, forgiveness, and faith lead to the Cross. The Cross points to our brothers. Jesus is present wherever there is a gathering in His name. The power of forgiveness is there too; there, the heart of one who is troubled can free itself of all its load of sin, by opening up and telling everything in trust to someone appointed by the Church.

—Heini Arnold

Healing for the Homosexual

Helpful Guidelines

by Ed Hurst

DON'T GIVE IN. Every day in our lives we are faced with choices. Often the "pleasures of the moment" seem so much more real than God's promise to sustain us through the temptation. You wouldn't be the first Christian to see an occasion to sin and then long to give in "for just a little while."

DON'T TURN BACK. Piled up guilt, frustration, bitterness, and self-contempt coupled with any failure can be hooks that Satan uses to lure you back into a life of sin. If thoughts of turning back grip you, ask God for wisdom to see what it is that's REALLY bothering you. "Search me, O God, and know my heart. Try me and know my thoughts. See if there be any wicked way in me and lead me in the way everlasting."

DON'T RUN ON YOUR OWN STEAM. So many times when I have found myself "in the pits" it's because I've been trying to run on my own power. I get so busy that I don't find time to pray or read the Bible. I hear thoughts like, "Can't read the Word now, I've got to catch up on the correspondence," running through my head. It takes only a day or two of this neglect for me to experience a noticeable weakening in my spirit. It is good to remember that "the life that I now live, I live by the faith in the Son of God."

DON'T LOOK FOR INSTANT ANSWERS. It is so easy for us to assume that once God has turned His spotlight on a needy area in our life, that area is settled once and for all. That's just the beginning. God desires to build patience in us through the "testimony of our faith," through "trials and temptation." We keep learning the answers more deeply as we grow in Jesus. God sometimes provides an instant answer so that men might see His power. More often He molds us into His image DAILY that men might see His character.

DON'T DEPEND ON FORMULAS. The only sure remedy for sin is the sacrifice of Jesus Christ. Beyond that, men may have different ideas about the roots of sin, confession, and repentance, the need for inner healing, deliverance, and discipleship. Each of these things are valid ways of dealing with sin, but whenever any one of them turns into a formula, the effectiveness dwindles drastically.

DON'T BUILD WALLS. The most common root of sexual sin is rejection. The most common response to rejection is to develop defense mechanisms that keep us from getting hurt. They also keep us from being helped. Learn to see yourself as a vital part of the Body of Christ. Let the rest of the Body get to know you a bit.

DON'T SETTLE FOR LESS THAN GOD'S BEST. For many of us, we were down so low that almost anything is an improvement. We tend to measure things by comparison. For instance, if I used to be suicidal, and now I'm only depressed 98% of the time, then I've really made some progress. But the fact remains that I'd still have a long way to go. There are a number of areas in our lives where we might be tempted to say "I've arrived," or "This is it. This is God's place for me." It's good to remind ourselves that He is able to do exceeding abundantly above all that we can ask or think before we settle in too comfortably on some plateau that we've mistaken for a mountaintop.

DON'T LOSE PERSPECTIVE. Remember that God sees all sin—from self-righteousness to sexual immorality, from lying to lusting—through the same eyes. The eternal consequences are the same. But He sees all of those who have been washed in the blood of His Son—regardless of their sin background—through the same eyes, too. These to Him are all dear sons and daughters, precious children, covered with robes of righteousness.

DON'T FORGET WHO YOU ARE. Your new identity is CHRISTIAN, which means "follower of Christ." Don't be deceived into focusing on one area of your past and thinking that this is who you are. Every single Christian, past, present, and future, has the same standing. We are all ex-sinners, ex-children of darkness. We need to forget about the former things and press on toward the mark of the high calling in Christ Jesus.

DON'T LOSE SIGHT OF JESUS. This one sounds so simple,

doesn't it? How many times have you heard it? How many times have you NEEDED to hear it? Haven't you noticed that when the problems start, it's usually when you've gotten upset or frazzled and your focus is on your feelings rather than on Him? Or you panic over some situation and you forget to turn to Him? Or you're feeling condemned and you're ashamed to talk to Him?

Sometimes people let you down, one after another, over and over again. Because you can't reach them, you kick at Him. Sometimes the pity-party feels so comforting that you'd rather wallow in it for awhile. And sometimes you get so caught up with "being a Christian" or "living by the book" that you're only going through the motions. You're not really living by His strength.

Oftentimes people can block your view of Jesus. Perhaps it's an ex-lover. Perhaps it's a Christian friend who you feel you couldn't live without. Or a pastor, counselor, or minister who has played an important role in your life. It could even be a church, a fellowship, or a denomination. Regardless of who it is or how strong a role they have had in your life, Jesus must come first.

It's very easy to lose sight of Him. It's even easier to see how quickly our old carnal nature surfaces when we do. We have to make this the central theme of our Christian walk—keeping our eyes on Jesus. I am convinced that Satan will use whatever tactics possible—whether it be guilt, sin, worry, or anxiety; fear, self-pity, personality conflicts, daily hassles, urgent tasks, or any other number of things—to distract us or to break our communion with Jesus. Our goal, once we've realized that the communion has been broken, is to restore it as soon as possible.

I have found that whatever the circumstances are, He has always been waiting with outstretched arms when I have returned from my journey into self and the pressures of the day-to-day routine. I have found that "the steadfast love of the Lord never ceases. His mercy never comes to an end. They are new every morning. . . . Great is His faithfulness!"

I trust that you have found or will find the same.

Ed Hurst is on the staff of Outpost Ministries, a group devoted to people struggling with homosexuality. If you would like help or more information, write to them at 1821 University Avenue, S-292, St. Paul, MN 55104 or call (612) 645-2530. They have a monthly newsletter available free on request.

CULTS

The Deadly Cults
An Ex-Moonie Looks Back

by John Rhodes

"THE MOONIES? I'd never get involved with them." You don't think so? Don't say that too lightly. The first time I had contact with the Moonies their belief and life-style did not attract me in the least. I was sure I would never fall for this Korean madman. But I underestimated the power of this group to use and exploit my own uncertainty about basic questions in life and my driving need to find answers. I *was* impressed by the sincerity and loving concern of these Moon devotees. That was my undoing. It will be yours too if you do not realize that behind the "loving" smiles is a plan to enslave your soul to the twisted purposes of one man's self-glory. Don't scoff at their power. Moon has already hoodwinked many prominent politicians, businessmen, and religious leaders. You may be next.

I grew up in the late '60s and, like many young people in that time, experienced a crisis of values. I groped to find the meaning of life and my place in it. I became disillusioned and depressed with my own life and with life around me.

My parents were at a loss to understand me. As children of the Depression and World War II, they had worked hard to provide economic security for us children. Protected from the struggle for economic survival, the children of my generation rejected the middle-class lifestyle of our parents to pursue the "meaning of life." Potentially this movement could have led to a deep spiritual renewal. Unfortunately, elements of violence, drugs, immorality, and occultism brought many to their ruin. In this spiritual vacuum the cults offered a way out.

The appeal of cults is not that they indulge the flesh but that they demand total sacrifice. There is a deep need in us all to live for a cause higher than ourselves.

In the Unification Church there were no drugs or sex. Instead I found a reason to live, a cause to fight for which demanded every ounce of my energy. This is why cults' recruiting practices are primarily aimed toward well-adjusted middle-class kids with a potential for leadership and sacrificial service. Young proselytes are rewarded with a comprehensive world view and a task in life that they could not find in modern middle-class society or in church.

In this sense the success of the cults is an indictment of our society. A shallow pleasure-principle pervades everything and turns off, depresses, or frustrates what is best in a young person. Cults exploit a genuine and honest seeking in young people.

As a Moonie, I was completely sure that I was living for God and His cause on earth. At first, the work of the Unification Church looked good. But that "good" is wolfishness in sheep's wool, darkness disguised as light. This makes the evil nature of the Unification Church difficult to discern because it appears as goodness and light.

The essence of Unification Church belief is that Sun Myung Moon is the Messiah, the Lord of the Second Advent. The essence of their life-style is obedience to him. Their

When I gave my life over to Moon, I placed my soul in the hands of dark powers.

theology, the "Divine Principle," is nothing more than a superficial interpretation of the Bible and history aimed at establishing Moon as the awaited Messiah. They do not accept the divinity of Christ. They write off the redemptive act of the Cross as a failure and manage to justify the very obvious human failings of Mr. Moon without losing their faith in him as the Messiah.

The Unification Church is a satanic imitation of what the Christian Church should be. True Christianity demands absolute obedience to the will of Jesus. The Unification Church substitutes Moon for Jesus and asks for the same obedience. Herein lies the source of its power. It is not just a collection of ideas and beliefs.

When I gave my life over to Moon, I placed my soul in the hands of dark powers. No amount of reasoning, no matter how sound, could have convinced me to leave the Unification Church. Attempts at "deprogramming" would have had no effect.

Now, I could list one by one all the errors in the "Divine Principle." But this does not break the power of Moon. Only Jesus can do that. This is not an intellectual debate over beliefs but a spiritual fight with dark powers that want to enslave your soul.

There is only one way to free yourself of these powers. A

higher power—Jesus Christ—must drive them out. If a person leaves the Unification Church without this experience of inner freeing he will find himself, at best, just as lost as he was before joining. More likely he will be worse off than before—he will probably be completely disillusioned about any dedication to God and will jump at the first opportunity to lead a selfish life. Either way Satan has his day. I doubt if such a person really does become free of Moon—deep inside he may feel he is unfaithful to the "cause." An incomplete break with Moon is no break at all. I am thankful that a decisive confrontation with Jesus marked my departure from the Unification Church. Without it I would have sunk into despair.

Your calling and mine is to give ourselves entirely to God. Pursuing individual happiness or sacrificing to false gods does violence to this calling. Jesus can free us from ourselves and from satanic powers. His cause is more demanding and more fulfilling than any of the cheap imitations offered by the false christs who walk the earth.

John Rhodes was majoring in psychology at the University of Maryland with no definite career in mind ("I was trying to find myself") when the Moonies found him. The son of a CIA employee, John lacked nothing but a sense of purpose in life. After leaving the Moonies in 1973, he joined the Hutterian Brethren, going from "night to day, or antichrist- to Christ-centered living."

HELP & HOPE

"Whoever Comes To Me I Will Never Turn Away"

—John 6:37

by Johann Christoph Blumhardt

WHEN THE LORD SEES SOMEONE COMING to Him, He does not ask who it is before receiving him. He is thrilled simply that someone is coming. And the more wretched the man is, the more is God's heart broken and the greater is His joy. He would never think of turning him away. He could not.

It is the same with us: we would sooner send away a healthy, strong man when we have given him what he needed than send away one who is miserable, ill, and quite helpless. How much more is it so with our dear Savior. The more helpless we are when we come, the less He can turn us away. "Whoever comes to me," He says. Nothing more. Simply

the fact that someone is *coming* is enough.

In what does this coming consist? When our spirit turns to God, that is the beginning. Jesus enters our thoughts only when we have become quiet, reflective, and considerate. Then, instinctively, we will push on: "O Lord, do not leave me." This is possible only for the broken heart, the humble heart. Merely the thought of Jesus and the longing to approach Him can break our hearts. All we can do then is come to Him in repentance and humility and talk to Him, entreat Him.

No one can come to Jesus with a defiant heart. He who prays stands at the threshhold of conversion. At least at that moment, he is broken. One does not need to preach to such a man. And we make a mistake if we reproach him for his sins—he might regret that he came.

We must learn to consider it an important event every time we meet someone, every time someone comes to us. Do not turn anyone away too quickly, even if it is awkward or a nuisance, before you have proved you can love. Much may depend on it. Remember, your Savior turns away no one who comes to Him. You should love as He does, as He accepts sinners.

If someone comes, he already loves the Savior, he has already surrendered to Him. So whoever comes to Him is worthy of Him. Just give yourself now wholly to Him and you will soon have Him with all His comforting love.

Take note, you wavering, doubting child. Run to Him in complete trust. He accepts you and does all he can for you. He gives it slowly, just as you need it, but in the end He gives you everything!

Johann Christoph Blumhardt was a 19th-century pastor who ministered to hundreds of people at his communal retreat in Bad Boll, Germany.

Freedom from Sinful Thoughts
A Review of the Book

by Howard R. Macy

I STILL REMEMBER THE VERBAL BATTLES my high school buddies and I fought over sin. Undaunted by the fact that we were theological novices, we baited and challenged each other and stubbornly defended our views. "Every day in a thousand ways we sin in thought, word, and deed," they argued, almost too blithely, I thought. "No," I countered, "that's arguing for sin and giving up on genuine Christian living." Though we never found common ground on the answer, we readily admitted common ground on the problems, one of which was the reality of temptation and sinful thoughts in our daily lives. Is it sin to be tempted daily as we were? Is there any hope of overcoming the fascinating tug of impure thoughts, pride, anger, and other temptations? It is precisely these questions we shared which Heini Arnold so helpfully addresses in his book, *Freedom from Sinful Thoughts.*

Part of the good news Arnold brings us is that temptation in itself is not sin. After all, Jesus himself was tempted just as we are, according to the Book of Hebrews, and "if we dismiss the thought from our minds, we have not sinned—just as Jesus never sinned." Arnold warns pointedly that he is writing for those who want to be free of sinful thoughts, not for those who deliberately bring such temptations on themselves or wallow in them when they come. For those who are sincere, however, distinguishing between temptation and sin can begin to bring freedom.

In denying that temptation is sin, however, Arnold does not underestimate its power. We are up against all the forces of evil, he says, and they can be fully as subtle as they are powerful. Satan quoted Scripture to tempt Jesus and he often would deceive us as well with what is apparently good. Temptation has power also because it can come to us through many channels. Some thoughts come through "involuntary suggestions," impressions which may originate in movies, television, newspapers, and even childhood experiences. Other temptations may rise out of "autosuggestion" in which our fear of an evil idea may actually producc that idea in us. We may even come to such a point of "fascination" that evil thoughts have a special grip on us. To our frustration, the more we fight the thoughts that possess us, the more power they have.

How, then, can we overcome temptation if it is so powerful? Arnold suggests two basic steps. First, recognize that we cannot conquer evil on our own and that our well-meaning attempts through stubborn willpower often breed our own defeat. "Ultimately," Arnold writes, "all we have is our sin." Victory requires surrender. It means that we must come to God with a "completely empty heart."

Having admitted our own weakness, we must then rely completely on the power of Christ. This is the force of the book's subtitle, "Christ alone breaks the curse." We must believe that Jesus can and will do everything. One of the ways that Christ frees us is by replacing our own willpower with a deeper and more powerful will, "the real, essential desire or will of the heart," which is really "Christ . . . deep within our hearts." This is the willpower that emerges in victory, transformation, and purity of heart.

Arnold mentions on several occasions two practical steps in learning to rely on Christ. The first is honesty, "absolute truthfulness." He insists rightly that it hinders us to try to deceive God, ourselves, or each other. That is why confession is important and often needs to involve qualified members of the community of faith. The other step is "detachment." We must quiet our hearts daily as well as in the thick of trouble so that we can "hear the deeper voice within our own heart. We hear Jesus, who seeks us and loves us." The honest, quiet heart, then, becomes the arena of God's victory.

The book's closing pages unfold the grandeur of God's Kingdom and how we can come to feel "God's great plans in our hearts," plans with universal, even cosmic, significance. At first this vision seems only loosely related to sinful thoughts, but we are soon drawn out of our self-centeredness and cramped vision to see the magnificence of God's love and the totality of Christ's victory. Indeed, it is precisely because Christ has broken the power of sin throughout the creation that we can hope to have the freedom from sin we long for.

Freedom from Sinful Thoughts is a beautiful little book about a practical problem of Christian living. Because of Heini Arnold's loving, sensitive spirit, the reader feels encouraged rather than judged and better able to face up to the nagging problem of sin. At times Arnold's style seems sluggish (though always simple) and the examples from daily life too few. Nonetheless, there are many nuggets of practical wisdom, easily mined, that deserve to be read, pondered, and treasured. Arnold modestly proposes that in this book he hopes "to offer help to those who earnestly want to fight against sinful thoughts and who long to receive a completely pure heart." I am sure that for me and for many others he has done exactly that.

FREEDOM FROM SINFUL THOUGHTS: Christ Alone Breaks the Curse, Heini Arnold, Plough, 1973, 118 pp.

Howard R. Macy is Professor of Bible and Religion at Friends University, Wichita, Kansas.

Recommended Resources

Though not everything following reflects the exact views of the publishers, all of these resources offer excellent advice and encouragement.

For Teens

Alcoholics Anonymous: The Story of How Many Thousands of Men and Women Have Recovered from Alcoholism, third edition; New York: Alcoholics Anonymous World Services, Inc., 1976. This is AA's "Big Book"—their basic text. For a complete listing of AA publications, write AA World Services, Inc., Box 569, Grand Central Station, New York, NY 10163.

The Courage to Be Chaste by Benedict J. Groeschel, O.F.M.Cap.; Mahwah, NJ: Paulist, 1985.

Dear Doc . . .: The Noted Authority Answers Your Questions on Drinking and Drugs by Joseph A Pursch, M.D.; Minneapolis: CompCare, 1985.

Do You Sometimes Feel Like a Nobody? by Tim Stafford; Wheaton, IL: Tyndale House, 1980.

Toma Tells it Straight with Love by David Toma with Irv Levey; New York: JAN Publishing, 1981.

You Can Make a Difference by Tony Campolo; Waco, TX: Word Books, 1984.

For Parents and Youth Workers

All Grown Up and No Place to Go: Teenagers in Crisis by David Elkind; Reading, MA: Addison-Wesley, 1984.

Called to Care: Youth Ministry for the Church by Doug Stevens; Grand Rapids, MI: Zondervan, 1985.

The Complete Youth Ministry Cassette Library: A 30 Audio Cassette Resource Album. To order, write Word Church Services, P.O. Box 1790, Waco, TX 76796.

Dying for a Drink: What You Should Know About Alcoholism by Anderson Spickard, M.D., and Barbara R. Thompson; Waco, TX: Word Books, 1985.

Fatal Choice: The Teenage Suicide Crisis by John Q. Baucom; Chicago: Moody, 1986.

Four Arguments for the *Elimination* of Television by Jerry Mander; New York: Quill, 1978.

Ideas by Wayne Rice and Mike Yaconelli. As of 1986 there were 40 volumes (40-60 pages each) available from Youth Specialties, 1224 Greenfield Drive, El Cajon, CA 92021.

Ideas for Social Action: A Handbook of Mission and Service for Christian Young People by Anthony Campolo; El Cajon, CA: Youth Specialties, 1983.

Parents and Teenagers: A Guide to Solving Problems and Building Relationships, edited by Jay Kesler; Wheaton, IL: Victor Books, 1984.

The Plug-in Drug: Television, Children, and the Family by Marie Winn; New York: Viking, 1977. Also published in 1978 by Bantam Books.

Resource Directory for Youth Workers edited by Jim Hancock; Grand Rapids, MI: Zondervan.

Toughlove Solutions by Phyllis York, David York, and Ted Wachtel; New York: Bantam, 1985.

What About Crime?: Constructive Approaches to Violence by Kit Kuperstock; Scottdale, PA: Herald Press, 1985.

Stories of People Who Won Out Over Problems

The Autobiography of Malcolm X by Malcolm X; New York: Ballantine, 1977.

Black Boy by Richard Wright; New York: Harper & Row, 1969.

Born Again by Charles Colson; Old Tappan, NJ: Fleming H. Revell, 1977.

Bruchko by Bruce Olson; Wheaton, IL: Creation House, 1978.

Child of Rage by Glenn Hester and Bruce Nygren; Nashville: Thomas Nelson, 1981.

Diary of a Young Girl by Anne Frank; Garden City, NY: Doubleday, 1967.

The Honorable Alcoholic: A Senator's Personal Story by Harold E. Hughes with Dick Schneider; Grand Rapids, MI: Chosen Books. (Formerly published as *The Man from Ida Grove.*) 1979.

Life Sentence by Charles Colson; Old Tappan, NJ: Fleming H. Revell, 1979.

The Man Who Keeps Going to Jail by John R. Erwin; Elgin, IL: David C. Cook, 1978.

Miracle on the River Kwai by Ernest Gordon; Wheaton, IL: Tyndale House, 1984.

My Shadow Ran Fast by Bill Sands; New York: Signet, 1964.

They Called Me the Catch-Me Killer by Bob Erler with John C. Souter; Wheaton, IL: Tyndale House, 1981.

Three Gates to Hell by Jim Tucker with Virginia Koehler and Don Tanner; Costa Mesa, CA: Gift Publications, 1980.

Twice Pardoned: An Ex-con Talks to Parents and Teens by Harold Morris with Dianne Barker; Arcadia, CA: Focus on the Family, 1986.

Acknowledgments

The publication of this booklet was made possible by the help and cooperation of many, many people. Special thanks go to Sarah Darden and the staff at *Cornerstone* magazine, Mike Yaconelli, Barbara Thompson, Tony Campolo, and all the others who worked over the manuscript and offered us their advice and suggestions.

For their help and support we thank Superintendent Carl Berry, Volunteer Services Supervisor Charles Davis, Protestant Chaplain Hector Chiesa, and Commercial Art Instructor Morris Marcus of the Woodbourne Correctional Facility (see "About the Artists"). And for help with the printing, thanks go to Superintendent Louis Mann, Deputy Superintendent of Programs Paul Levine, Education Director Winston Gandy, Volunteer Services Supervisor Jeff Rubin, Vocational Supervisor Tullio Santarelli, Printing Instructor Bruce Freer, and the 34 inmates of the Shawangunk Correctional Facility print shop.

Thanks to Judge Karen Peters, Howard Macy, and Walter Wilson for the work you submitted.

Finally, we want to thank the following publishers and authors who gave us permission to reprint their material:

The words of the Russian visitor to the U.S. quoted in "TV Robotics" are taken from *The Improbable Triumvirate* by Norman Cousins and reprinted by permission of the publisher, W.W. Norton & Co.

The quotations from *Four Arguments for the Elimination of Television* by Jerry Mander are printed by permission of William Morrow & Co. Copyright © 1977, 1978 by Jerry Mander.

The quotations from *The Plug-In Drug* by Marie Winn are printed by permission of Viking Penguin. Copyright © 1977 by Marie Winn Miller.

"The Innocent Drug" is condensed from *Toma Tells It Straight with Love* by David Toma with Irv Levey, JAN Publishing, 1983, and printed with David Toma's permission.

"Life with an Alcoholic" appeared originally in *Focus on the Family* and is reprinted in part with permission of the author.

"The Honorable Alcoholic" is condensed from *The Honorable Alcoholic: A Senator's Personal Story* by Harold E. Hughes with Dick Schneider, Chosen Books, 1979 and printed by permission of Harold Hughes.

The quotations by Michael Segell are from *Rolling Stone*, May 31, 1979 by Straight Arrow Publishers, Inc. © 1979. All rights reserved. Reprinted by permission.

The quotations by Anderson Spickard and Barbara Thompson are reprinted from *Dying for a Drink* by Anderson Spickard, M.D. and Barbara R. Thompson, copyright © 1985 and used by permission of Word Books, Publisher, Waco, Texas.

"The 12 Steps of AA" are reprinted by permission of Alcoholics Anonymous World Services, Inc.

"Loving the Unborn Child" is taken from a speech by Mother Teresa given at the National Right-to-Life Convention in July 1985.

"There Is Help Out There" is taken from an article in *Seventeen*, April 1979, and is printed by permission of the author.

The quotation by Anne-Grace Scheinin on suicide is taken from "The Burden of Suicide," *Newsweek*, February 7, 1983, copyright © 1983 by *Newsweek* and reprinted by permission.

"Schools Must Help Prevent These Tragedies" by Pamela Cantor appeared originally in the February 26, 1986, issue of *USA Today*. Copyright, 1986 *USA Today*. Excerpted with permission.

"The Challenge of a Changed Life" is reprinted by permission of the author from *Cornerstone* magazine.

"Healing for the Homosexual" appeared originally in *Outpost*, the newsletter of Outpost Ministries and is reprinted by permission.

"Whoever Comes to Me I Will Never Turn Away" is translated and condensed from the reading for April 10 in *Er Sandte Sein Wort*, Freimund-Verlag, 1974.

The publisher has sought to locate and secure permission for the inclusion of all copyright material in this booklet. If any such acknowledgments have been inadvertently omitted, the publisher would appreciate receiving the information so that proper credit may be given in any future printings.

This book has been made possible by the cooperation of many authors. Every effort has been made to include only reliable information. The publishers would welcome knowing about possible omissions or errors.

The publishers do not necessarily endorse all the positions of the authors or organizations represented in this booklet.

About the Artists

Jdern "Foxx" Lybrand grew up in New York City. He has been drawing for over 30 years. The week he completed the drawings for this publication, he came before the parole board and was approved for release. He was home for Christmas, 1986, after six years in prison.

Stevie Moore is serving a five-year sentence in the New York State prison system. He grew up in Manhattan where he attended the Art and Design high school followed by an 18-month course at the Pels School of Arts. Stevie is up for parole in 1989.

Morris Marcus, left, is Woodbourne Correctional Facility's commercial art instructor.